For more resources, companion guides, or to contact the author, visit:
www.kathrinshaffer.com

Printed in Canada

First Edition

Right-ish

Trying to Live Holy Without Losing Your Mind

Dedication

To my children –

You've taught me more about love, forgiveness, and grace than you'll ever know. I pray that my life, though imperfect, always point you to the One who is perfect. May you walk in truth, guided by the light of Christ, all the days of your life.

To the new believer who feels behind or unworthy –

You're not too late, and you're not too far gone. God's grace is wide enough for all our regrets and deep enough for every need. This book is for you.

And above all,

To my Savior, Jesus Christ

You rescued me. You restored me.

You are the reason I write, the reason I live, and the only One worthy of all my praise.

Acknowledgement

Writing this book has been one of the most humbling and faith-building experiences of my life, and I couldn't have done it alone.

First and foremost, I thank my Lord and Savior, Jesus Christ. You found me when I wasn't even looking. You loved me when I was still running. Every page of this book is a testimony of Your grace, Your patience, and Your transforming power in my life. To You be all the glory.

To my husband – thank you for walking with me through every season, before I knew Christ, and now as I'm learning to walk with Him daily. Your love has been a steady anchor in my life, a reflection of God's faithfulness even when I didn't always see it.

You've believed in me when I doubted myself. You've been patient as I've grown, encouraged me when I felt inadequate, and supported me as I stepped into something completely new and unfamiliar. Your quiet strength and unwavering commitments have been a gift from God to me.

Thank you for the prayers you've prayed behind the scenes, the sacrifices you've made without complaint, and the way you've allowed me the space to become the woman God is shaping me to be. I couldn't have written this without your love beside me.

To my children. Thank you for your love, your strength, and your patience with me as I've grown in my faith. You've watched me change, stumble, and rise again. I hope this book reminds you of how deeply I love you, and even more, how much Jesus does.

To the friends and mentors who prayed with me, encouraged me, and reminded me of truth when I doubted, your support has been the quiet strength behind every chapter. Thank you for being the hands and feet of Christ in my life.

To my church family, you've walked with me through the earliest days of my faith, through the joy and through tears. Thank you for showing me what Christian community is supposed to look like: real, gracious, and rooted in love.

To every reader picking up this book – thank you. I don't take your time or trust lightly. My prayer is that these words stir your heart towards Jesus, draw you closer to His truth, and encourage you to live boldly, even when it's hard.

And finally, to those who think they're too late or too broken to be used by God – let this book be proof that He writes the most beautiful stories with surrendered hearts.

With all my heart,

Kathrin

Let's be honest: the phrase "Christian ethics" doesn't exactly send tingles down your spine. It sounds like the kind of phrase that belongs in a 400-page theology textbook, or a painfully awkward seminary lecture delivered by someone who thinks whiteboards and footnotes are spiritual gifts. You don't see people getting Christian ethics tattoos or naming their kids "Moral Responsibility." (At least I hope not.)

But before you scroll past this chapter like it's a list of Levitical dietary laws, stick with me.

Because believe it or not, Christian ethics is not about being a rule-following robot or saying "no" to everything remotely fun. It's not about becoming the "moral police" of your friend group. And it's definitely not about trying to impress God with how many sins you avoided last Tuesday.

Christian ethics is actually something wild, freeing, and astonishingly relevant. It's not the dusty attic of the Christian life; it's the living room. The everyday space where faith turns into choices, beliefs turn into behaviour, and your walk with God puts on shoes and hits the road.

See, ethics is simply how you live out what you believe. And Christian ethics?

That's how you live as someone who belongs to Jesus, not just on Sunday's or when you're holding a Bible in your hand, but when you're stuck in traffic, shopping for toilet paper, or deciding whether or not to subtweet that person from Bible study who always "accidentally" monopolizes prayer requests with their life story.

Let's get one thing straight from the start: you already have ethics. You already live by some set of rules or values, even if they're mostly unspoken. Everybody does. Even the guy who double dips his chips at the church potluck has a working moral framework, it's just possibly terrible.

Some people base their ethics on feelings. "If it feels good, do it." Others base theirs on vibes, horoscopes, or inspirational quotes on kitchen towels. Some get theirs from Grandma, who warned them that dancing was the devil's playground (but never quite explained why church picnics still had line dancing). Some folks even create a Frankenstein code of conduct, a stitched-together mess of memes, talk show opinions, TikTok theology, and that one time they misunderstood something Jesus said in a parable and built a life philosophy around it.

But Christian ethics says, "Let's anchor this thing in something that doesn't move," Let's not try to invent right and wrong based on how we feel at 2 a.m. or what's trending on Instagram. Let's go to the source, God Himself.

That's right. Christian ethics isn't based on your mood, your preference, or your enneagram number. It's based on the character of God. Who He is. What He's revealing. How He's shown us to live, not just through commands, but through a Person: Jesus Christ.

This is huge. Because if God is holy, just, merciful, and loving, then we – His people - are meant to reflect those things in our decisions. That's not about rigid rule-keeping. It's about being transformed into someone who lives and loves like God does. It's not about winning "Christian of the Month." It's about living with the kind of moral clarity and compassion that makes people say, "Wow. There's something different about that person...and it's not just that they don't swear."

Now let's talk about the elephant in the pew: grace.

We love grace. We write songs about it. We put it on mugs. We whisper it to ourselves after we've eaten an entire bag of mini-donuts in one sitting.

But somewhere along the way, grace got pitted against ethics. Like they were opponents in a theological boxing match. On one side, you've got "Grace": arms wide open, singing kumbaya, letting people off the hook. On the other side, "Ethics": clipboard in hand, side-eyeing everyone and quoting Leviticus before breakfast.

Here's the thing: that's a false choice. Grace and ethics aren't enemies. They're partners. Grace is the fuel. Ethics is the road. Without grace, you're driving on empty. Without ethics, you're just revving the engine in neutral.

When Jesus forgave the woman caught in adultery, He didn't say, "It's fine. Go back to your thing." He said, "Go, and sin no more." That wasn't harsh, it was holy. He gave her grace and a new direction. That's what He does with all of us.

Christian ethics flows out of grace, not guilt. It's not a frantic attempt to earn God's love, it's the natural result of having already received it. You don't pursue holiness to get into heaven. You pursue holiness because heaven already got into you.

Still, let's acknowledge the struggle. Living out Christian ethics isn't easy. It's hard to be kind when people are infuriating. It's hard to tell the truth when a lie would be way more convenient.

It's hard to love your enemies when your enemies are also just really, really annoying.

Sometimes, you don't want to reflect Jesus. You want to reflect a sassier, more sarcastic version of yourself. One who doesn't turn the other cheek, but turns up the volume and the shade.

But that's why we need more than just effort, we need transformation.

You don't become ethical by following rules better. You become ethical by following Jesus closer.

And the more you walk with Him, the more you change. Slowly. Clumsily. Miraculously. You become less reactive and more compassionate. Less self-centered and more servant-hearted. Less addicted to being right and more devoted to being righteous.

This isn't behaviour modification. It's heart transformation.

It's not about taping good fruit onto a bad tree. It's about becoming a new tree altogether. Rooted in God's truth. Watered by His Spirit. Bearing the kind of fruit, love, joy, peace, kindness, and the rest, that only grows in someone who's surrendered to grace.

The truth is, Christian ethics doesn't give you a map with a route that avoids all pain.

It gives you a compass pointing to true north, even when the road is messy and full of potholes.

It's what tells you to show up with integrity when no one else is. To forgive when you'd rather block them. To speak truth when silence is easier. To give when it costs you. To love when it hurts.

And no, it won't always make you popular. Ethical living rarely trends. But it will make you holy. It will make you whole. It will make you look just a little more like Jesus.

And that? That's worth everything.

But let's get even more practical. What does this actually look like when the rubber hits the road – and by "road," I mean the place where people cut you off and your sanctification is tested?

Christian ethics doesn't just exist in ivory towers and quiet time journals. It lives in conversations, conflicts, and the chaos of real life. It's the part of your faith that speaks up when someone's being gossiped about in a prayer group. It's what steps in when you're tempted to take shortcuts at work or fudge your taxes "just a little." It's what reminds you that God is watching – not in a creepy surveillance kind of way, but in a "you're still mine, act like it" kind of way.

The problem is, we live in a world that has made ethical compromise look...normal. Expected. Even applauded.

Cutting corners is clever. Bending truth is strategic. Doing what benefits you most is called "self-care," even if it means ghosting your responsibilities, ditching your commitments, or walking away from people God told you to love.

But Christian ethics calls us to a higher standard, not because we want to be different, but because we already are. We are citizens of another Kingdom. Ambassadors of a holy God. Lights in a dark world. Salt that hasn't lost its saltiness. And if we don't live like that matters, the world around us won't either.

Now, this doesn't mean we live with a moral superiority complex. Please don't. Nobody needs another Christian acting like they're God's moral accountant, keeping track of everyone else's sins while ignoring their own pride and passive-aggression. (Jesus had a few things to say about people like that, and none of them involved handing out gold stars.)

What it does mean is that we live with conviction. Quiet, steady, courageous conviction that says, "I belong to Jesus, and I'm going to live like it – even when it's inconvenient, unpopular, or misunderstood."

There will be tension. Ethical living always brings it.

You'll feel it when you're tempted to laugh at a cruel joke but something inside you says, "This isn't honoring."

You'll feel it when your friends say, "Just date whoever you want," but you're trying to honor God with your relationships.

You'll feel it when you're choosing between extra profit and doing what's fair.

You'll feel it when you want to clap back online but instead choose silence – or worse, kindness.

Let's be real. There are moments when Christian ethics feels like carrying around a "Make Things Harder for Myself" button. You say no when others say yes. You hold your tongue when others go off. You give when you're not required to. You forgive when the world says, "Cut them off and never look back."

Why?

Because you're not following the world's example. You're following Jesus.

And here's the real kicker: sometimes the hardest part isn't choosing between right and wrong, it's choosing between what's permissible and what's Christlike.

Because grace doesn't just free you from sin. It frees you to rise above what's merely acceptable and into what's holy. That's where Christian ethics really starts to glow in the dark. It's the difference between living clean and living surrendered.

So, let's talk about Jesus for a minute; because He's not just our Savior. He's, our standard.

People love to quote Jesus when He says things like, "Come to me, all who are weary." Or "Judge not, that you be not judged." (Especially if they're being called out on something.) But Jesus also said things like, "Love your enemies," and "Take up your cross," and "If your right hand causes you to sin, cut it off."

Not exactly bumper sticker material.

Jesus didn't come to give us a motivational speech. He came to redefine everything. The way we think. The way we live. The way we treat people we don't like.

He didn't lower the bar of ethics. He raised it and then gave us His Spirit so we could actually start clearing it. He didn't say, "Do better." He said, "Follow Me."

That's Christian ethics in its purest form: living as Jesus would if He had your job, your family, your schedule, your temptation, and your location. Living like Jesus would if He were you.

That's a tall order. I mean, Jesus never dealt with traffic or social media trolls or family group texts that never die.

But He did face betrayal. Misunderstanding. Pressure. Injustice. Loneliness. Physical pain. Public scrutiny. Temptation. And in all of it, He stayed sinless. Holy. Loving. True.

So no, Christian ethics isn't about being a good person. It's about becoming like Jesus.

It's about letting the Holy Spirit remake you so thoroughly that your life starts to echo Christ's even when you're not trying. So that your integrity shows up in your taxes. Your compassion shows up in your conversations. Your holiness shows up in how you carry yourself on a date. Your peace shows up in how you respond to conflict.

And before you say, "That sounds impossible," let me say: you're right. On your own, it totally is. That's why God didn't just save you – He filled you.

He gave you, His Spirit. He put a new heart in you. And every day, that Spirit is gently, consistently shaping you to look more like Jesus. That's sanctification, in case you want a theological word to throw around at brunch.

You don't wake up one day magically ethical. You wake up daily, choosing to walk in step with the One who is.

Some days you'll nail it. Some days you'll trip over your own attitude and faceplant into sarcasm and pride. But you get back up. You confess. You learn. You grow.

That's why Christian ethics doesn't demand perfection. It invites progress.

You don't need to fake it. You just need to follow. And the more you follow Jesus, the more natural it becomes to live like Him, even if it still takes a lot of reminders, do-overs, and "Lord, help me," prayers whispered under your breath while smiling through gritted teeth.

Christian ethics is not for people who have it all together. It's for people who are being held together by grace. Who fall seven times and get up eight. Who know they need mercy just as much as they're called to extend it.

It's for the real-life saints and the recovering sinners. The church kids who are just now realizing what they believe and the new believers who still say "dang" a little too hard.

It's for you. For me. For all of us learning what it means to live in the tension between grace and obedience, truth and love, boldness, and humility.

You don't have to be the perfect Christian.

You just have to keep showing up, keep surrendering, and keep saying, "Lord, I want to live like I'm Yours – today."

Here's something else they don't tell you in Sunday school: living ethically won't always win you friends.

In fact, if you're doing it right, there's a good chance it'll cost you something. Maybe popularity. Maybe invitations. Maybe the approval of people who think "doing what feels right" is the highest virtue.

The world isn't offended by vague spirituality. Post a Bible verse with a sunset and you'll get a few hearts and maybe a "Yaaas queen, amen." But live out that Bible verse – walk in forgiveness, tell the truth, say no to sin, call out injustice, love sacrificially – and suddenly you're "too intense," "too Christian," or "too judgemental."

Welcome to the tension of being a disciple in a world that would rather you be vague, agreeable version of yourself.

Christian ethics doesn't exist in a vacuum. It shows up in the middle of this culture noise, a world that celebrates tolerance until you disagree, demand freedom without accountability, and praises authenticity as long as it's comfortable.

And in that world, ethical Christians will stand out.

Not because we're yelling louder. Not because we're smug about being right. But because we carry a quiet, holy resistance in the way we live. We forgive when others gossip. We serve when others step back. We love the people nobody else wants to love. We don't just talk about justice – we embody it.

It's not performative. It's not about being "the good Christian" in the group. It's about being so anchored in Christ that your choices start to reflect heaven instead of whatever's trending that week.

The truth is, most people won't read a Bible before they read your life. And that should sober us. Because while God's grace is more than enough for our failures, the way we live still speaks. Loudly.

When our ethics align with God's character, we become a walking billboard for the gospel, living proof that transformation is real, that holiness isn't outdated, and that integrity is still powerful in a world full of compromise.

But when our ethics are wishy-washy? When we say we follow Jesus but live like everyone else? The message gets fuzzy. People start asking, "If Jesus changes lives, why hasn't He changed yours?"

Ouch. But necessary.

That's why ethics matter. Not just to keep us in check, but to shine light in the places where people are fumbling around in moral darkness.

And let's be clear: this kind of light isn't about being loud. It's not about being the morality police. It's about being so radically kind, so deeply truthful, so relentlessly gracious, so courageously honest, that people have to wonder what kind of God could produce a person like that.

That's the goal. Not perfection. Not applause. But a life that whispers (and sometimes shouts), "There's something different here. And it's not me. It's Him."

But here's the good news, you're not expected to generate this light on your own. God doesn't give you an ethics manual and says, "Good luck!" He gives you something better: the Holy Spirit.

And with the Spirit comes the fruit, not fruits, plural. One fruit, with all these beautiful, wild, transforming pieces that grow in you like unexpected blessings from a divine gardener.

Love. Joy. Peace. Patience. Kindness. Goodness. Faithfulness. Gentleness. Self-control.

Not just traits to strive for. Traits that begin to surface naturally the more time you spend walking with God.

This fruit isn't seasonal. It's supernatural. It shows up when your circumstances say it shouldn't. Love when you've been hurt. Joy when you're stressed. Peace when you're surrounded by chaos.

It doesn't mean you walk around like a Christian version of a yoga instructor, whispering "blessings" with a serene smile while your life burns behind you. It means you're steady. Anchored. Becoming someone who looks less like your past and more like your Savior.

But – let's be real – it doesn't happen overnight.

You don't go from a raging monster to serene saint just because you read Galatians once. You don't wake up with patience because you played worship music while brushing your teeth.

Fruit takes time. And pruning. And watering. And sometimes a bit of suffering, if we're honest. The kind of suffering that shakes loose the things you thought you needed, until what remains is something more pure, more Christlike, more enduring.

That's the heart of Christian ethics. Not slapping a Jesus sticker on your personality and calling it discipleship. But letting God do slow, holy work in you that changes how you think, how you respond, how you spend, how you serve, how you speak, and how you love.

It's slow. It's not always glamorous. But it's deeply good.

And you'll start to notice the shift.

You'll catch yourself pausing before replying with that biting comment.

You'll apologize sooner.

You'll give when it hurts.

You'll stay when it's easier to walk away.

You'll bite your tongue when you could have told them off with poetic precision.

You'll choose obedience over applause.

And not because you're trying to impress God – but because you know He's already impressed His love on you.

That's how it works. Grace changes your "have to" into a "want to."

Suddenly it's not "I have to do the right thing," It's "I want to honor the One who's been so good to me."

And sure, you'll still mess it up. You'll still say things you regret and make decisions you'll have to untangle with prayer, repentance, and possibly baked goods if you need to make peace with someone. (Cookies: the unofficial sacrament of forgiveness.)

But you'll keep growing. You'll learn from your mistakes. You'll become more aware of God's presence in your everyday choices. You'll see how small decisions add up to a transformed life. And one day, you'll look back and realize you don't react like you used to. You don't chase the things you used to. You don't fake peace – you actually have it.

That's ethics done right. Not performative morality. But a deep, inward shift that shows up in outward choices.

It's not about being holier-than-thou. It's about being holier-than-you-were-last-year.

That's the progress we're after. Not spiritual superiority, but consistent surrender.

That's what makes ethics come alive. Not memorizing rules but becoming someone who reflects the rule-giver. Someone who's still messy, still growing, but genuinely transformed.

And when people see that? They'll start to wonder.

Not "What makes you so good?"

But "Who's made you like this?"

And that's your moment. Not to preach. Not to brag. But to point back – humbly, honestly, joyfully – to the One who's been shaping your life behind the scenes all along.

Here's the part no one puts on a t-shirt: you will fail at this.

You're going to mess up.

You're going to lose your temper when you swore you were working on patience. You're going to say the wrong thing, sometimes out loud, sometimes in a group chat. You're going to choose comfort when you were called to courage. You're going to give in to pride when humility was knocking.

Even with the best intentions, even with daily devotions, even with your favorite worship playlist on repeat, you will stumble.

And here's the miracle: God already knows.

He's not shocked by your failures. He's not redoing His plan because you forgot to read Leviticus this year. He's not pacing in heaven, muttering, "Well, I guess we have to throw the whole sanctification process out now."

No. He's still here. Still forming you. Still working on your heart like the patient, relentless craftsman He's always been.

Because Christian ethics was never about performing perfection. It's about pursuing Jesus.

And that pursuit will come with scraped knees, ugly tears, awkward apologies, and a trail of "I didn't mean to, but I did."

And all of it is covered by the grace of a God who doesn't run when you fall, He kneels beside you, helps you up, and says, "Let's keep going."

You're not measured by how often you fail. You're being formed by how often you let God pick you up, cleanse you, and send you back into the world a little wiser, a little softer, a little more surrendered than you were before.

The enemy would love to convince you that the moment you fail, you've disqualified yourself from holy living.

But God says, "That moment? That's where I start the next chapter."

And this is why repentance is one of the most powerful tools in the life of a believer, not because it resets the scoreboard, but because it reorients your heart.

When you repent, you're not groveling to earn God's love. You're returning to it.

You're saying, "God, I want to live like I'm Yours. I want my actions to line up with my identity. Help me walk in that again."

It's realignment, not rejection.

That's why Christian ethics includes room for confession.

Because the path of holiness isn't a perfectly paved road, it's a trail of daily, hourly decisions to come back to Jesus. Again and again.

And with every return, you become a little more like Him.

So don't let failure make you cynical. Let it make you humble. Let it make you merciful. Let it break down your pride and deepen your empathy.

Because nothing makes you more compassionate toward someone else's struggle than remembering your own.

You're not above failing. None of us are.

But you are held by the same grace that raised Jesus from the grave.

And that means you're not done yet.

Now let's circle back to something crucial. Because as we talk about ethics and transformation and all these high-level spiritual concepts, there's a temptation to think, "This is a me thing. I have to get this right."

But here's the secret: this isn't a solo mission.

Christian ethics is not a personal DIY project. It's not spiritual IKEA furniture you assemble alone while crying and wondering where you lost the second bolt of patience and the tiny wrench of wisdom.

This is a community project. You grow in ethics with other people, through church, discipleship, accountability, friendship, and yes, sometimes through really difficult relationships that test every ounce of your sanctification.

You don't get more ethical by hiding away with your Bible and a candle. You get more ethical when you're bumping into other sinners who are also trying to become saints.

You learn patience when someone tests yours. You learn honesty when it would cost you something. You learn humility when someone else gets the thing you prayed for. You learn forgiveness when the wound is still fresh, and the apology never came.

This is where the good stuff happens. Not in isolation. In interaction.

Because ethics isn't proven in theory. It's proven in tension.

Anyone can be peaceful alone. But try being peaceful at a family reunion during an election year. That's where you find out what's really growing in you.

That's also why the Church is such a vital space for ethical growth. It's not a perfect space, but it's a holy one. And it's full of people just like you; trying, failing, repenting, forgiving, growing.

You're not just accountable to God. You're accountable to one another. Because your ethical life doesn't just affect you. It affects the witness of the Body of Christ.

People are watching, not judging you, but to see if this whole Jesus thing actually works.

They want to know if following Him makes any difference when it comes to how you live, love, and show up.

You might be the only gospel someone ever hears. The only ethics lesson they get. The only picture of Jesus they'll see before they decide whether or not He's worth trusting.

That's not pressure. That's purpose.

That's the joy of ethical living. Not that it makes you feel good about yourself, but that it puts Jesus on display in everyday, ordinary decisions.

That's what makes it holy.

Let's not sugarcoat it though: living this way will stretch you.

You'll have to go first in peacemaking. You'll have to risk being misunderstood. You'll have to stop defending yourself when your flesh is screaming for vindication. You'll have to live out the Sermon on the Mount in a world that thinks meekness is weakness, mercy is naive, and purity is prudishness.

But you won't be alone. God is with you. His Spirit is in you. His Church surrounds you. And His Word will keep you steady.

You're not just trying to live well. You're becoming someone new.

Someone who can face pressure without folding, who can walk into chaos with peace, who can lose status and still stand tall in righteousness. Someone who can be wronged and not retaliate, who can love without strings, give without applause, serve without resentment.

That kind of person doesn't just happen.

That kind of person is formed; by grace, by truth, by the Holy Spirit, and by daily decisions that align with the God you serve.

And the more you make those decisions, the more it becomes second nature. Not because you're pretending to be holy, but because holiness is growing in you from the inside out.

That's the heart of Christian ethics.

It's not a religious mask.

It's a holy mirror, showing the world what Jesus looks like in the skin of someone who's still figuring it out, still stumbling forward, but still committed to walking in the light.

Let's talk about one of the most uncomfortable aspects of Christian ethics, you're going to look weird.

Not in a "wear a Jesus fish suit and hand out tracts at the mall" kind of weird. (Please don't.) But in a countercultural, upside-down Kingdom kind of way.

Because the more your ethics reflect Jesus, the less they'll resemble the moral norms of the world around you. And that's not an accident – it's the plan.

You'll start noticing that the stuff Jesus praised; meekness, mercy, peacemaking, self-denial, doesn't exactly make the cover of Forbes or get the most views on YouTube.

You'll feel the tension when your coworkers celebrate ambition without accountability, when influencers sell self-indulgence as self-care, and when "your truth" is treated like it's sacred, even if it directly contradicts someone else's.

This is where Christian ethics digs its heels in an says:

"No. We don't follow that compass."

We live by a different map. One that calls the first last and the last first. One that says giving is better than hoarding, serving is better than being served, and dying to yourself is the path of life.

This is what Jesus meant when He said things that make modern audiences squirm:

"Blessed are the poor in spirit. Blessed are they that mourn. Blessed are the meek. Blessed are they which are persecuted for righteousness' sake..." (see Matthew 5)

It's a list that, by worldly standards, sound like a tragedy. But to Jesus, it's the beginning of blessing. Because Christian ethics isn't about getting ahead in this world; it's about being ready for the next one.

It doesn't mean you walk around trying to be disliked. That's not holiness – that's just bad social skills.

But it does mean you'll make decisions that confuse people. You'll show mercy when others demand revenge. You'll admit wrongs instead of hiding them. You'll resist the impulse to clap back, when it feels so good.

And sometimes, that obedience will cost you. You might be passed over. You might lose friends. You might be misunderstood, mocked, or labeled as "too much."

But take heart. You're in good company.

Christian ethics means choosing faithfulness over favor.

It means knowing that your audience is God – not the comment section, not your boss, not even your family. You answer to One. You live for One. And when that One says, "Well done," it makes every sacrifice worth it.

And let's be clear – it is a sacrifice.

We're not pretending this is easy. Nobody naturally wakes up wanting to forgive their enemies and pray for their betrayers. (If you do, please check for a pulse. You may be an actual angel.)

This kind of living goes against the grain of your flesh and the pull of your culture. It costs pride. Comfort. Convenience.

But it also gives back more than it takes.

Because when you start walking in ethical alignment with God's character, you gain something no Instagram quote can give you:

Peace.

Not the fake peace that comes from numbing your feelings or winning arguments. Real peace. The peace of walking in step with your Savior.

That's the peace you can sleep on. A peace that holds you steady in storms. A peace that anchors your yes and no. A peace that speaks louder than approval.

And here's what's wild: people notice.

Even if they don't understand your theology. Even if they don't agree with your convictions. Even if they think your beliefs are outdated or extreme – they will notice your peace. Your consistency. Your integrity.

And that's often the seed that leads to conversations. Not because you tried to "win" someone. But because you lived in a way that made them hungry for the God who makes people like you.

Christian ethics isn't just about avoiding sin. It's about revealing God.

It's about living in such a way that people don't just hear the gospel, they see it. Not perfectly, but clearly. Not loudly, but powerfully.

They see it when you're wronged and respond with humility. When you could cheat but choose honesty. When you could gossip but guard someone's reputation instead. When you could ghost, rage, or lie, but instead; you love.

And they'll ask themselves, even if they never say it out loud: "Who are these people?"

That's your cue. Not to preach – but to point.

To quietly, humbly, and joyfully point them to the One who changed your heart, rewrote your values, and gave you the power to live differently.

That's what ethics does. It clears the fog around the gospel. It shows people that Jesus isn't just a belief system, He's a living, active King whose values can be seen in your calendar, your credit card statement, your screen time, and your search history.

This is what makes ethics so important. Not because it earns you salvation. But because it shows that salvation is already at work.

Because the truth is, you can't fake this stuff for long. You can't white-knuckle your way into Christlike living. Eventually, your default settings will show. The pressure will reveal what's real. And that's a good thing.

Pressure is where ethics collapses or shines.

In pressure, you find out if your integrity is anchored or borrowed. If your generosity is real or performative. If your faith is built on conviction or convenience.

And here's the gift: God is not grading you. He's growing you.

He uses the pressure. The mess. The moral crossroads. Not to humiliate you, but to form Christ in you.

And if that sounds overwhelming, remember this: you are not alone. You never have been. The same God who saved you is now working in you.

Shaping your choices. Refining your reactions. Guiding your thoughts.

Not with condemnation. With peace.

And all along the way, He's whispering:

"Keep going. We're getting there."

Because Christian ethics isn't a destination. It's a direction. A journey. A daily return to the One who is holy, loving, just, and true, and who calls you to walk in His way, not so you can be impressive, but so you can be whole.

You are becoming someone new.

Right-ish. Faithful-ish. Holier than yesterday, not as holy as tomorrow.

And God, in all His grace, is smiling the whole day.

Let's talk about what nobody posts on Instagram: the painfully slow pace of spiritual growth.

Because here's the truth about Christian ethics that rarely makes the highlight reel: most of the time, it's quiet. It's ordinary. It's so subtle, you almost miss it.

You won't always feel holy when you're making the right decision. You won't get a standing ovation for not sending that passive-aggressive email.

There won't be confetti raining down when you apologize first, tip generously, or choose forgiveness instead of revenge.

Christian ethics won't always feel epic. But it will feel...anchoring. Like something real is being built under your feet, choice by choice, even when it doesn't seem glamorous.

This is the unsexy, underrated magic of consistency. The spiritual superpower of simply showing up.

Because guess what? Most of your formation won't happen during revival meetings or "mountaintop moments." It'll happen while you're washing dishes, replying to emails, doing school drop-offs, or choosing not to blast someone on Facebook.

God is forming you in the mundane.

He's working in your ordinary rhythms – the way you speak to your kids, the tone you use with your spouse, the patience you show at the grocery store when the self-checkout malfunctions for the third time, and a small part of you wants to lose your salvation, right there in front of the Tic Tacs.

He's there. Refining. Sanding. Shaping.

That's what makes Christian ethics so powerful. It's not about epic, dramatic decisions (though sometimes it includes those).

It's about daily decisions. Hundreds of small ones. The kind nobody notices – but God sees them all.

He sees when you bite your tongue. When you shut off the gossip. When you delete the angry post before you hit send. When you text to check on someone instead of judging them from a distance. When you choose quiet obedience instead of attention-seeking religion.

And none of it is wasted.

Every time you align your actions with God's truth, even if it costs you comfort, visibility, or immediate gratification, you're training your heart to reflect His.

It might not go viral, but it goes deep.

And the deeper it goes, the steadier you become. The kind of person who isn't blown over by every emotion, every insult, every temptation. The kind of person who, over time, begins to look like Jesus without even realizing it.

That's how real transformation works. Not all at once. But inch by inch.

You'll catch yourself doing the right thing when no one's watching. You'll realize you're more patient than you used to be. You'll start to feel conviction sooner. You'll say "I'm sorry" faster. You'll stop defending the version of yourself that grace is trying to heal.

And when that happens, don't rush past it. Celebrate it.

It's okay to rejoice when growth shows up. It's okay to say, "Hey, I didn't handle that like I used to." That's not pride. That's progress That's evidence that God is at work.

Of course, not every day will feel like a win. Some days you'll fumble the ball. You'll say the wrong thing, choose the easy way out, or sit in bitterness instead of offering grace.

But here's the promise: the Spirit is still working.

He hasn't left. He hasn't given up. He's not throwing up His hands saying, "This one's hopeless."

No. He's whispering, "Let's get back up. Let's try again."

And in that trying again, over, and over, you become someone new.

That's the real heart of Christian ethics. Not behaviour management, but soul formation.

You're not just becoming a better version of yourself. You're becoming a reflection of Jesus.

And the world desperately needs more of that. Not more perfect people. Not more opinionated Christians. Not more religious influencers.

The world needs more people who walk like Jesus – quietly, consistently, faithfully. People who carry peace into chaos. Who carry kindness into conflict. Who carry light into the shadows and grace into the broken places.

And here's the secret: you can be that person.

Not because you're naturally amazing, but because God is supernaturally faithful.

You don't need a seminary degree. You don't need to have it all figured out. You just need a heart that's willing to keep saying yes.

Yes, to truth. Yes, to love. Yes, to repentance. Yes, to accountability. Yes, to surrender.

That kind of yes has power. That kind of yes will change the way you live, the way you lead, the way you love. And not just for a season. For a lifetime.

So, keep going. Keep choosing the hard right over the easy wrong. Keep showing up in the small moments. Keep asking the Holy Spirit to make you into the kind of person who honors God – even when no one's watching.

Because someone is watching.

And one day, they might ask you, "How do you live like that? What makes you different?"

And you'll get to smile and say, "It's not me. It's Jesus. I'm just trying to walk with Him."

And in that moment – messy, unpolished, and maybe a little awkward – you'll become a living example of what Christian ethics was always meant to be:

A testimony.

Not of your goodness, but of God's transforming grace.

If Christian ethics stayed in the "thoughts and prayers" realm, it'd be easier. We'd just nod along during sermons, feel a little convicted, maybe tear up during a worship song, and call it a day.

But Christian ethics doesn't stay put. It moves into every room of your life. Even the messy ones you've been trying to keep locked since 2003.

It's not just how you vote or how you treat people at church. It's how you handle money. How you set boundaries. How you respond when someone cuts you off in traffic and then waves like you were the problem.

It's the digital life, how you speak online, what you consume, what you post, and what you scroll past like it doesn't affect your heart.

It's your ambition, how you define success, how you climb ladders, how you treat people on the way up and down.

It's your relationships, your family, your friendships, your dating life, your marriage.

It's your sexuality, your integrity, your generosity, your humor, your habits.

In short: Christian ethics is whole-life ethics.

There is no area of your life that the Spirit is uninterested in transforming. He's not just doing character work in your Sunday persona. He wants your Tuesday attitude, your Thursday choices, and your Saturday night honesty.

You can't compartmentalize holiness. You can't keep Jesus in a spiritual glovebox and only pull Him out when things go sideways. He's not your emergency contact. He's your King.

And if He's your King, then every part of your life becomes His territory.

That might sound overwhelming. Honestly? It is. But it's also wildly freeing.

Because when Jesus reigns in every part of your life, you don't have to juggle masks. You don't have to wonder which version of yourself you need to be in each room. You become someone whole. Someone consistent. Someone real.

And that's incredibly rare.

In a world where everyone's curating their image and performing for different audiences, a person of integrity – a person whose ethics match their beliefs – is a revolutionary act.

You don't need to be impressive. Just true.

But here's the challenge: the deeper Jesus moves into your life, the more things He starts rearranging.

He might ask for your schedule. He might challenge your spending. He might tap on your attitude toward authority. He might gently, but firmly, say, "We're not going to carry that bitterness anymore."

And if you're anything like the rest of us, your flesh will fight back.

Because we love the idea of transformation – right up until it costs us something.

Right up until obedience means we don't get the last word. Or we have to give up the relationship. Or we forgive before we apologize. Or we say "no" to the thing that would've made us look good but wasn't right.

This is the friction of Christian ethics. It's not in the concepts; it's in the choices.

And sometimes, those choices will go against everything your culture tells you to value.

Sometimes they'll go against everything you thought you valued.

But this is where you discover something amazing:

God's way is better.

Always.

It's not always easier. It's not always faster. But it's truer. And in the end, it's more fruitful.

You'll see it in your relationships. In your peace of mind. In your character. In your clarity. In your trust in God, not just as Savior, but as Lord.

Because as you choose holiness over hype, obedience over opinion, and truth over trend, something changes.

You stop needing everyone's approval. You stop living for applause. You stop fearing man because your fear of God has become your anchor.

And that kind of person? That kind of person shakes the gates of hell.

Not because they're loud. Not because they're perfect. But because they are faithful.

And Christian ethics is faithfully in action.

It's not just choosing right over wrong. It's about choosing Jesus over everything else, again and again, until it's not just a discipline but a delight.

You'll find yourself waking up thinking, "Lord, I want to walk with You today, not just believe in You, not just sing about You, but live like You."

And when that desire takes root, something extraordinary begins to grow.

You start to hate sin, not because you're scared of getting caught, but because you love the One who saved you from it. You start to hunger for righteousness, not to earn God's favor, but because you already have it, and now you want to live like it. You start to recognize how your little decisions are shaping your witness, not out of paranoia, but out of purpose.

You realize this isn't about impressing God. You can't. He's already infinitely holy and unimpressed by our resume of "mostly good behaviour."

This is about responding to love with love.

About answering grace with surrender. About showing up each day and saying, "Lord, what would You have me do today that reflects who You are and who I belong to?"

And that changes everything.

Suddenly ethics isn't a list of rules. It's a relational response. A daily choice to live in such a way that if someone followed you around with a notepad, they'd catch glimpses of the Kingdom, unexpected moments of mercy, truth, beauty, sacrifice, and love that all point upward.

They might not even know it's Jesus at first. But they'll know there's something different.

And eventually, they'll ask.

That's your moment. Not to puff up your chest and say, "Well, I just really try to be a good person."

No. That's your chance to say, "I'm actually not a good person on my own. But Jesus is. And He's been changing me, one messy, miraculous day at a time.

Let's land the plane.

After all this talk about ethics, daily choices, character formation, gospel witness, holiness over hype, it's fair to ask: What if I don't feel like I am doing a great job?

What if, instead of being a beacon of holy consistency, you feel more like a flickering candle in a wind tunnel?

What if you've read this chapter and thought, "Well...that's adorable.

But I just snapped at my kid, lied on a form, scrolled past three gossip posts, and liked one of them. I'm not even the ethical person my dog thinks I am."

Welcome. You're in good company.

Because none of this is about pretending, we're crushing it. It's about recognizing that grace is what carries us through the gap between who we are and who we're becoming.

Christian ethics doesn't ignore the mess. It meets us in it, and says, "Let's start here."

Maybe your ethics feels inconsistent. Maybe your life has chapters that don't read very holy. Maybe you're still struggling with stuff you thought would be gone by now.

Gods not panicked.

He's not shocked by your humility. He's not threatened by your inconsistency. He's not giving up because you've needed to say "sorry" for the same thing seventeen times this month.

He is, however, inviting you. Always. Again and again.

Inviting you to live like someone who's already loved. Inviting you to become someone who embodies His Kingdom, here and now. Inviting you to walk in a way that makes heaven visible in a very messy world.

You're not doing this for Him. You're doing this with Him.

That's the game-changer.

Because without Him, ethics becomes exhausting. It becomes a treadmill of spiritual striving, where you measure your worth by your performance and burn out before you even reach February.

But with Him, it's not performance, it's partnership.

It's waking up each day and saying, "Lord, I don't have this all figured out. But I want to walk with You. I want to live in a way that reflects you. I want to be a living, breathing echo of Your truth and grace, even if today all I managed is a whisper."

And God honors that whisper.

He's not waiting for you to master morality. He's asking you to keep coming back to Him. To stay in the light, even when it shows the dust. To trust that His Spirit is doing work in you that's slower than you'd like, but deeper than you imagined.

Because here's the secret: transformation rarely feels impressive while it's happening.

It's easy to look around and think everyone else is farther along. More ethical. More self-controlled. More peaceful. More consistent.

Don't buy it.

What you're seeing is fruit at a distance. You don't see the wrestling. The tears. The 3 a.m. prayers. The repentance. The counseling. The journals full of scribbles that say, "God, help me be different."

Everyone is being formed. You're not late. You're not behind. You're just in progress.

And that's beautiful.

Because ethics isn't just about arriving at "right." It's about becoming righteous-ish, more like Jesus each day, even if it's in tiny, hard-won steps.

Even if your best today is just pausing before you snap, or admitting you were wrong, or choosing silence when you're tempted to self-justify.

Even if all you did today was not give in to bitterness, that counts.

Because when you live from grace, progress is enough. You don't have to be perfect. You just have to keep going.

Keep letting the Word shape you. Keep asking the Spirit to guide you. Keep leaning into a Church that challenges you. Keep showing up to the hard stuff with a soft heart. Keep choosing light over shadows.

And when you mess it up – and you will – don't run from God. Run to Him.

Let repentance be the rhythm of your life, not the exception. Let confession be a doorway to intimacy, not a signal of failure. Let grace be your banner, not your excuse.

Because this is the journey. Not of becoming morally superior, but of becoming spiritually surrendered.

So, when someone asks, "What is Christian ethics, really?" you'll be able to say, with humility and a knowing smile:

It's learning to live like Jesus; awkwardly at first, but more naturally over time – by grace, through faith, with a lot of help from the Holy Spirit and coffee.

It's becoming the kind of person who tells the truth when it would be easier to lie, who forgives when it would be easier to punish, who serves when it would be easier to hide.

It's ordinary holiness. Invisible faithfulness. Behind-the-scenes righteousness. All rooted in the overwhelming goodness of a God who not only calls us to live well but equips us to do it.

And friend, you can do it.

You really can.

Because God is not just commanding you, He's empowering you.

He's not just telling you how to live, He's living in you.

So, breathe deep. Shake off the shame. Pick up your cross. And let today be another step toward becoming the person Jesus already knows you're capable of becoming.

Not because you're great. But because He is.

And He's not done with you yet.

Not even close.

God as the Standard

(a.k.a. "Be Holy Like God – Which Sounds Cute Until You Try It")

Let's start with an uncomfortable truth that we all sort of know but don't love admitting out loud:

You are not the moral gold standard.

I know, you might be lovely. You recycle, you say "bless you" when someone sneezes, you've maybe even baked banana bread for a neighbor without expecting a thank-you note or a Grammy nomination.

But even on the best day, when your coffee hits just right, the traffic is light, and your kids call you "the best" without being sarcastic, you're still not the standard.

Neither am I. (Ask anyone who's seen me before 8 a.m. or after two back-to-back Zoom meetings.)

And yet, that's the way most of us operate when it comes to ethics. We start with us. Our feelings, our instincts, our experiences, our sense of what's fair. We build our moral compass out of the mood boards and TikTok trends and the occasional Bible verse we half-remember from a youth group skit in 2007.

The problem? Our inner compass isn't just off – it's wobbly.

It swings wildly depending on what benefits us, who we're around, or whether we're hangry. (Let's be real: it's hard to love your neighbor when you haven't had lunch.)

That's why Christian ethics doesn't begin with you, me, your favorite pastor, or even a theology book. It starts with God.

Specifically, it starts with God's character.

And that's a whole different ballgame. Because God isn't wobbly. He's not moody. He's not updating His standards every time culture invents a new hashtag.

He is unchanging, eternally good, perfectly holy, and the source of all that is right.

His character doesn't just define morality, it is morality.

So, when we talk about living ethically as Christians, we're not asking, "What reflects the heart of God?"

Because God's character isn't just some theological concept to study, it's the foundation we're supposed to stand on.

Think of it this way: God isn't just asking you to be holy for the aesthetic. He's inviting you to reflect Him. And that's both beautiful...and terrifying.

"Be ye holy; for I am holy." 1 Peter 1:16

Okay. But what does that even mean?

Holiness isn't just "don't do bad things." It's not about wearing long skirts, avoiding R-rated movies, or never laughing at a sarcastic meme. Holiness is about being set apart, different, distinct, shaped by the character of God rather than the culture around us.

Which brings us to the big, uncomfortable realization:

God's standard is so much higher than ours.

He doesn't grade on a curve. He doesn't go, "Well, you meant well, so close enough." He doesn't tally up the good vibes and subtract the oopsies.

He is the standard. The absolute, unchanging, blindingly pure standard.

That might sound overwhelming. Honestly? It is. But it's also really, really good news.

Because if God were anything less than perfect, we'd be in trouble. Imagine a God who was just kind of moral. Mostly good. Generally truthful. Occasionally faithful. You wouldn't be able to trust Him with your life, your pain, or your identity.

But the God of Scripture is never "mostly." He's always completely. Completely just. Completely merciful. Completely holy. Completely wise. Completely loving.

Which is great...until you realize He's calling you to be like Him.

Not because He expects perfection overnight, but because that's what transformation actually looks like.

The goal isn't to become "better people." The goal is to be conformed to the image of Christ. (Romans 8:29, if you're curious.) And Christ is the exact representation of God's character in human form.

So...no pressure or anything.

But here's the thing; God doesn't leave us to guess what He's like. He reveals His character clearly. Through Scripture. Through the person of Jesus. Through the conviction of the Spirit. Through creation. Through His justice and His mercy and His bizarre patience with people like Jonah and, let's be honest, you and me.

And when you study His character, you start to realize something:

His ethical expectations aren't arbitrary – they're deeply personal.

He calls us to forgive not because it's easy, but because He forgives. He calls us to love our enemies not because it makes sense, but because He loved us when we were still enemies. He calls us to tell the truth because He cannot lie.

He calls us to be faithful because He is always faithful, even when we're flakey and forgetful.

God's character is the blueprint of Christian ethics. And when we ignore that blueprint, things get weird fast.

We start making our own definitions of love, definitions that involve warm feelings but not sacrifice. We redefine justice, usually in ways that make us feel better and someone else feel punished. We talk about kindness, but only toward people who already agree with us. We praise humility, as long as we're not the ones being humbled.

Without God's character as our anchor, we build ethical systems that look good on bumper stickers but fall apart in real life.

But with God's character as the foundation? Everything changes.

Suddenly, ethics isn't about what works – it's about what honors Him.

It's not about being liked – it's about being aligned.

It's not about looking good – it's about looking more like Christ.

And slowly, quietly, steadily, that alignment starts to shape you. You start to say no to things you used to justify.

You start to crave righteousness instead of revenge. You start to feel uncomfortable with the compromises that used to feel normal.

You start to live like someone who belongs to a holy God.

And when you do? People notice. They may not understand it. They may not applaud it. But they will see it.

And that's the point.

Because at the end of the day, your ethical life is not about impressing the world. It's about reflecting the One who saved it.

Once you start to realize that God Himself is the moral standard, you'll probably have a moment of low-key panic. Something like:

"Wait…if God is perfectly holy, and I'm…well, me, then how in the world am I supposed to live up to that?"

That's a fair question. Because at first glance, the character of God feels less like a goal and more like a mountain range – breathtaking, impossible to climb, and filled with avalanche warnings.

But let's slow down.

Yes, God is holy. Absolutely, unapologetically, irreversibly holy. And yes, you are not. Also, absolutely. But, and this is big, God never expected you to become holy without Him.

That's the gospel – shape twist: the One who sets the standard is also the One who meets you in the inability to reach it.

He doesn't lower the bar. He lifts you.

He doesn't say, "Here's the perfect blueprint, good luck." He says, "Walk with Me, and I'll shape you as we go."

That's the beautiful tension of Christian ethics. We're not called to reflect God's character from a distance like we're copying off His heavenly homework. We're invited to walk with Him closely, so consistently, that over time, His character starts rubbing off on ours.

We call that sanctification, the Spirit's long, loving, frustrating, faithful process of making you look less like your sin and more like your Savior.

It's not a sprint. It's more like a road trip with a toddler: slow, filled with random detours, surprising joy, and occasional fits of "Are we there yet?"

But it's real. It's happening. And the end goal isn't behaviour modification – it's Christlikeness.

Let's break it down with a metaphor. (Jesus loved metaphors, so we're in good company.)

Imagine your life is a mirror. When God made humanity, He designed us to reflect his image. That's in Genesis, Day One type stuff.

It's what gave humans value, dignity, and purpose. We were made to mirror God's character to the world – justice, truth, mercy, beauty, creativity, relationality, love.

But sin didn't just smudge the mirror. It shattered it. So now, instead of reflecting God's character clearly, we reflect it in fragments.

What sanctification does, and what Christian ethics reinforces, is this slow, sacred process of putting the mirror back together.

And not with glue. With grace.

It's not a perfect reconstruction. Not yet. But every time you choose truth over convenience, every time you offer kindness instead of sarcasm, every time you choose humility over pride, you're letting the light of God shine a little more clearly through your life.

And the world needs that light.

Because make no mistake: we are living in a moral fog.

Our culture is saturated with conflicting messages about right and wrong, good and evil, truth and opinion. Ethics is not a buffet line – pick what works for you, skip what doesn't, and don't you dare judge someone else's plate.

But Christian ethics says, "Nope. We're not building a morality of preference. We're reflecting a Person."

And the Person we're reflecting doesn't shift with the trends.

God's character is not "vibe-based." It's not reactive. He's not flipping His standards every few decades to keep up with the cultural moment. His holiness is eternal, and that's what makes Him trustworthy.

You never have to wonder if God's love is real. If His justice is fair. If His patience is a front. You don't have to worry that He's going to cancel you mid-prayer because you stumbled again.

His character is consistent. And that consistency becomes your foundation.

Because when you know what God is like, you stop guessing what righteousness looks like. You know.

You stop trying to manufacture goodness and start mirroring it. You stop looking for loopholes and start leaning into the Spirit. You stop faking fruit and start growing it.

That's the shift.

And yes, its uncomfortable. Because the more you see God's holiness, the more you see your lack of it.

This is what happened to Isaiah, the prophet. You know, the guy who wrote a whole book in the Bible and had visions of heaven and probably had a pretty solid prayer life.

Even he saw God and basically collapsed into a puddle of "Woe is me."

"Woe is me! For I am undone; because I am a man of unclean lips..." -Isaiah 6:5

And you know what God did?

He didn't say, "Wow, Isaiah. What a letdown."

He didn't hand him a self-help scroll and say, "Come back when you've fixed your lips."

He cleansed him. He called him. He sent him.

That's what God does when we encounter His holiness. He doesn't shame us – He transforms us.

Not through pressure, but through presence.

So, when you start to feel like a moral failure next to God's perfection, remember: conviction is not condemnation. It's an invitation to go deeper.

It's the Spirit saying, "Hey, there's more. Let Me grow you. Let Me clean this area. Let Me make this part of you look like Jesus."

And if you say yes to that process, even imperfectly, you're walking the path of true Christian ethics.

A path paved not by guilt or religion, but by grace and glory.

So, let's go a little deeper.

If God is the standard, then who He is, becomes the filter through which we define every ethical decision. And the good news is, He hasn't hidden His character. We don't have to guess or invent what He's like. He tells us.

Let's start with a few greatest hits. You've probably heard these before, but let's slow them down, and see how they land when we apply them to our everyday lives.

First up:

"God is love." (1 John 4:8, just in case you need receipts.)

This one gets quoted a lot, on mugs, t-shirts, bumper stickers, even on soft-focus social media posts featuring sunsets and baby goats. But let's be honest: "God is love" has been hijacked so often that it sometimes ends up sounding like "God is chill" or "God is whatever makes you feel nice."

But that's not the kind of love we're talking about.

God's love isn't passive, mushy, or blindly affirming. It's active, sacrificial, and fiercely holy. It's the kind of love that moves toward sinners without enabling sin. The kind that corrects because it cares. The kind that says, "I will die in your place so you can live."

When we say God is love, we mean that everything He does is motivated by a pure, righteous, others-centered commitment to the good of His people and the glory of His name.

So, what does that mean for us?

It means our ethics must also be motivated by love – not ego, not fear, not legalism.

It means we don't speak the truth to shame people; we speak it to set them free. It means we don't "love" people by coddling them into destruction, we love them by telling the truth in grace. It means we don't just post about justice, we embody it, because love always seeks what is right.

Next one:

"God is just." (Deuteronomy 32:4: "a God of truth and without iniquity, just and right is he.")

This one makes people a little nervous. We like the idea of God being loving. Just...less excited about Him being just.

Because justice implies standards. Consequences. Accountability. And if you've ever had to return something without a receipt, you know how allergic our culture is to accountability.

But God's justice is not some angry lightning bolt factory. It's the foundation of everything good.

You want God to be just. You want Him to care about evil. You want Him to stand up for the oppressed. You want Him to deal with wickedness, not just wink at it.

Without justice, love becomes indulgence. Ethics becomes chaos. Everything unravels.

So, when we reflect the justice of God, we're not becoming harsh, we're becoming honest.

We're acknowledging that some things are not okay. That not every choice is valid. That righteousness matters.

And we begin to act accordingly. We stop excusing corruption. We stop calling sin "a lifestyle." We stop confusing forgiveness with silence.

God's justice calls us to act on behalf of the vulnerable, to speak truth in the face of power, and to repent when we're the ones on the wrong side of right.

That's hard. But it's holy.

Let's keep going:

"God is merciful." (Psalm 103:8: "The Lord is merciful and gracious, slow to anger, and plenteous in mercy.")

Now we're talking. Mercy is the warm blanket of God's character – the thing that keeps us from being consumed by the consequences we deserve.

God's mercy means He doesn't immediately drop the hammer when we mess up. It means He withholds judgement long enough for us to repent. It means he sees our brokenness and doesn't recoil; He moves toward it.

And if we're called to reflect that?

That changes how we treat people.

It means we give the benefit of the doubt. It means we remember our own flaws before we attack someone else's. It means we stop acting like we're the Holy Spirit's bouncers and start becoming the kind of people who show compassion in the middle of someone else's mess.

Mercy doesn't mean compromise on truth, it means delivering it with kindness.

It means seeing someone who's stuck and saying, "I've been there too. Let me walk with you."

Now – deep breath – let's talk about one more attribute:

"God is truth." (John 14:6, Jesus said it plain: "I am way, the truth, and the life.")

This one is especially spicy in our culture.

Because truth is no longer viewed as objective, it's now personalized, individualized, and optional. We're moved from "Tell the truth" to "Tell your truth," which often translates to, "Say what you want and hope no one checks the math."

But God doesn't operate in half-truths, spin, or rebranding. He doesn't manipulate. He doesn't gaslight. He doesn't fudge the numbers to make Himself look better.

He is truth. And He calls us to walk in truth.

That means we tell the truth even when it's awkward. We live in truth even when it costs us popularity. We defend truth even when the world rolls its eyes.

Truth is not harsh. But it is solid. It's the thing you can build your life on without fear that it'll collapse in a storm.

So, when we reflect the truth of God, we become people of clarity, not confusion. People of integrity, not image.

People who can be trusted – because we don't change our tune when the spotlight shifts.

And that's rare.

But that's exactly what Christian ethics is meant to produce, people who reflect the love, justice, mercy, and truth of God in a world that's desperately confused about all four.

Have you noticed that everything around us is always changing?

Fashion, slang, phone models, coffee sizes, online etiquette; it's all on a constant spin cycle. What was trendy last year is cringe this year. What was "brave" in one decade is "problematic" the next. Even what counts as a vegetable seems negotiable now, (looking at you, cauliflower pizza crust.)

And when everything is shifting, there's a quiet panic that starts to set in. A question we don't always say out loud, but we feel it: What am I supposed to stand on?

That's where the character of God comes in like a deep breath of mountain air.

Because while everything else spins, God does not.

He is immutable. (Big theology word. Basically, means unchangeable. Like your grandma's fruitcake recipe, but significantly more trustworthy.)

God doesn't grow, evolve, drift, or morph. He doesn't update His moral code like a smartphone OS. There are no patches, fixes, or beta versions of God.

The same God who parted the Red Sea is the one who comforts you at 2 a.m. The same God who gave Moses the law is the one who gives you grace when you blow it. The same God who judged nations is the one who gently convicts your heart when your sarcasm gets a little too spicy.

That consistency? It's not boring. It's foundational.

Because when you're building an ethical life – when you're trying to navigate hard choices, complex people, and confusing moments – you need a constant.

And you have one.

"For I am the Lord, I change not..." Malachi 3:6

That one verse? It should probably be your lock screen wallpaper. Because it's easy to forget. It's easy to believe that God has maybe softened over the centuries. Or that He's too loving now to care about sin. Or too kind to confront us.

But no. He's the same. Same holiness. Same mercy. Same wrath. Same patience. Same grace.

And that's what gives your life ethical clarity.

Because instead of wondering, "What's right in this moment?" you can ask, "What reflects the God who never changes?"

Not what feels trendy. Not what gets most likes. Not what causes the least resistance. What reflects Him.

That question – asked with sincerity and humility – has the power to transform everything:

How you speak to your spouse when you're both tired.

How you respond when someone offends you online.

How you spend money when no one's watching.

How you act at work when everyone else is cutting corners.

Because again, Christian ethics isn't about being nice. It's about being anchored.

Its' about becoming a walking preview of God's character. A little window into what love-with-standards looks like. A living reminder that goodness isn't extinct; it's just rare.

And that's the kind of rarity that stands out.

When you're consistent in your integrity, people may not always thank you, but they'll trust you. When you're steady in your compassion, people might test you, but they'll confide in you. When your yes means yes and your no means no, people may be surprised, but they'll respect you.

And that doesn't just happen by trying harder.

It happens by rooting yourself in who God is – not just once, but daily.

Think of it like brushing your spiritual teeth. You don't do it once and call it a lifetime. You come back to the same truth over and over:

God is holy. God is good. God is faithful. God is just. God is merciful. God is true.

And because that's who He is, it's who we are becoming.

But let's pause here and be real: this whole "becoming like God in character" thing? It can feel completely out of reach. You read the Gospels and watch Jesus gently restore a woman caught in sin or challenge the self-righteous without flinching, and you think, "That's awesome." I just made a passive-aggressive face in traffic and immediately regretted it."

Which is why we need to talk about one of the most underrated attributes of God:

God is patient.

So, patient.

He's not shocked when you fall short. He doesn't revoke your spiritual membership card when you misstep. He knows exactly how long this process of transformation will take, and He signed up for it anyway.

You're not the first slow learner. (The disciples say hello.)

Remember Peter? He was literally being mentored by Jesus in the flesh and still managed to deny Him three times in one night. Not once. Not twice. Three.

Did Jesus cancel him?

Nope. He restored him. Called him. Used him to build the Church.

Why? Because Jesus wasn't surprised by Peter's inconsistency. And he's not surprised by yours.

He's not looking for instant holiness. He's looking for surrender. For teachability. For willingness.

He can work with that. He is working with that.

So next time you feel like you're failing at this whole Christian ethics thing, remember it's not about achieving moral perfection. It's about walking faithfully with a God whose character is your compass and your comfort.

And when you stumble, (because you will), you don't start over. You keep walking. You keep listening. You keep letting His unchanging nature steady your ever-changing moods, habits, and heart.

Because slowly – but surely – you are becoming more like the One who never changes.

Let's talk about the dreaded ethical gray areas.

Because while some moral decisions are obvious, don't steal, don't cheat on your taxes, don't kick your neighbour's dog, others are, well…murkier.

What do you do when there's no specific Bible verse for your situation? No verse about how to handle that weird coworker, respond to your passive-aggressive aunt, or decide whether to go full influencer with your Christian baking TikTok?

This is where Christian ethics either goes shallow…or goes deep.

See, shallow ethics relies on rules alone. It wants a clear yes or no for everything, "Is it a sign or not?" becomes the guiding question.

And listen, rules are good. We love the rules. The Ten Commandments still slap.

But life isn't always as tidy as "Do this, not that."

Some decisions aren't about sin vs. obedience. They're about wisdom vs. foolishness, love vs. selfishness, or God's character vs. my convenience.

And this is where knowing God becomes your greatest ethical tool.

Because if His character is the standard, then when Scripture doesn't give you a direct command, His nature becomes your compass.

You ask:

"Is this aligned with God's justice?"

"Does this reflect His mercy?"

"Am I walking in truth or in pain?"

"Would a holy God call this wise?"

"Is love driving this decision – or is it fear, pride, or people-pleasing?"

Suddenly, ethics becomes less about external behaviour and more about internal alignment.

You stop trying to find the line you can toe without technically sinning. You stop asking, "How far is too far?" And you start asking, "How close can I walk with God in this?"

That shift changes everything.

You're not trying to obey a checklist. You're trying to reflect a Person.

It's not about perfection – it's about proximity.

Because when you're close to God, His heart rubs off on yours. And that changes the way you interpret those "gray zones."

Take speech, for example.

You're not going to find a verse that tells you whether you should subtweet that friend who ghosted you, or "politely destroy" someone in the comments section.

But you do know what God is like.

You know He's slow to anger. You know He delights in mercy. You know He values truth without cruelty. You know he doesn't trade sarcasm for sanctification.

So, you pause. You listen. And maybe – just maybe – you delete that post.

Not because you're trying to be a saint. But because you're trying to sound like your Father.

This is what maturity looks like. Not obsessing over what's allowed but longing for what's aligned.

And here's where it gets even better:

You don't do this discernment work alone.

Jesus promised that the Holy Spirit would guide us into truth. Not just theological truth but ethical truth. Practical truth. Everyday truth.

The Holy Spirit is the ultimate internal GPS. Not the kind that reroutes you passive-aggressively when you take a wrong turn ("recalculating...again..."), but the kind that gently nudges you with conviction, clarity, and wisdom.

You feel it when your heart tugs just before you gossip. You sense it when your conscience lights up during a compromise. You hear the whisper when you're tempted to justify what you know isn't in line with who God is.

That's not guilt. That's guidance.

That's the spirit doing His job – forming you, reminding you, shaping you to look like Jesus from the inside out.

Because again, Christian ethics isn't just what you do, it's who you're becoming.

You're becoming someone who makes ethical choices not just because they're "right," but because they're God-honoring.

And honoring God isn't just about checking the right boxes – it's about cherishing the relationship.

When you know His character, His gentleness, His faithfulness, His honesty, His holiness, it becomes way harder to live in ways that betray it.

And when you do stumble (because yes, that's still going to happen), it's not about spiraling into shame. It's about running to the God you now know more deeply, trusting His grace to pick you up and set you back on the path.

This is the slow, sacred dance of sanctification.

One moment of clarity at a time. One obedient "yes" at a time. One awkward act of righteousness when no one claps, but heaven smiles.

So, the next time you hit an ethical gray zone, try this:

Pause the panic. Not everything has to be answered in 30 seconds.

Ask the character questions. What do I know about who God is, and how does that shape this moment?

Invite the Spirit in. Literally ask, "Lord, help me reflect You right now."

Choose the option that aligns with His heart.
Even if it's harder. Even if it's slower. Even if no one notices.

And then – breathe.

You don't have to get it perfect. You just have to stay pointed toward the Person who is perfect.

That's ethics in motion.

That's what it looks like to live not by the world's standards, not by your moods, but by the eternal goodness of a God who is always the same and always enough.

Let's talk about ethics in community.

Because it's one thing to reflect God's character in private. It's another thing entirely to try doing that around actual people.

You know the ones I mean.

The passive-aggressive coworker. The neighbour who mows their lawn at 6 a.m. on Saturdays. The person on Facebook who seems to believe it's their spiritual gift to comment "Just saying" on everything you post.

Living by God's standards sounds noble, until someone gives you a reason not to.

And that's exactly when it matters most.

Because ethics isn't proved in theory. It's proven in relationships. Not the easy ones. Not the ones where everyone agrees with you, celebrates your growth, and gives you gold stars for your spiritual development. No, no. The real testing ground is the messy, human, complicated space where your reflex is not "WWJD" but "WWSYCD" – What Would Slightly Younger, Crankier You Do?"

But that's where formation happens.

Because God's standard doesn't shift when you're irritated. His character doesn't retreat when you're offended. His love, mercy, justice, and truth are not reserved for "good vibes only." They're meant to show up in conflict, in disagreement, and in discomfort.

Let's break it down.

God is love.

Which means your ethical life has to include love, even for people who make you roll your eyes so hard it qualifies as exercise.

God is merciful.

So, you extend mercy, even when someone absolutely deserves a verbal takedown and a group chat screenshot.

God is just.

So, you don't excuse wrongdoing, even when it would be easier to stay quiet and keep the peace.

God is patient.

So, you don't snap just because you're right. You bear with people. Gently. Consistently. Even if you have to start your prayer time with, "Lord, it's me again. Still trying not to scream."

These aren't surface-level niceties. They're deep, Spirit-empowering choices.

And honestly? They're some of the hardest ethical decisions you'll ever make, not because they're unclear, but because they go against everything your flesh wants to do.

Your flesh wants to retaliate. Your flesh wants to ghost them. Your flesh wants to clap back, shut down, or tell your side of the story first with dramatic flair and perfect lighting.

But God calls you to a different kind of posture.

Not weak. Not passive. But holy.

That means firm in truth, soft in tone, quick to forgive, slow to anger, and open to correction.

It means you don't weaponize righteousness to shame people, you wear it like armor to protect what's right.

It means when someone fails, you don't throw the first stone, you look in the mirror, pick up a towel, and ask, "How can I help restore this person?"

It means even when you confront sin, and yes, sometimes you should, you do it not to win a debate, but to win a heart.

That's what happens when ethics flows from the heart of God. It creates a new kind of person:

The one who speaks up when others stay silent but does it with grace. The one who sets boundaries without bitterness. The one who holds convictions without contempt. The one who says hard things without being harsh. The one who quietly makes peace when everyone else is looking for someone to blame.

You don't have to be loud to be holy. You don't have to be right to be kind. You don't' have to compromise truth to show compassion.

You just have to be anchored in the unchanging character of God, even when everything around you feels chaotic and unfair.

Because here's what no one tells you about ethics: it's relational glue.

When you live by God's standard you become someone safe to be around – even when people disagree with you.

You become trustworthy. Consistent. Humble enough to admit when you're wrong, bold enough to stand when you're right, and wise enough to know the difference.

And let me just say it – that kind of person is rare.

In a world that prizes outrage, sarcasm, and image management, someone who quietly honors God in their relationships is a walking revival.

It doesn't mean everyone will love you. Some might misunderstand you. Some might accuse you of being too soft, or too strong, or too principled, or not principled enough.

That's okay.

Because you're not living to reflect public opinion. You're living to reflect God.

And His approval isn't based on polls. It's based on His perfect knowledge of your heart.

So, when relationships get messy, and they will, don't measure your ethics by how easy the interaction was. Measure it by how faithfully you reflected your Father.

Did you love?

Did you tell the truth?

Did you protect the vulnerable?

Did you act justly and walk humbly?

Did you apologize when needed, and forgive even if it wasn't asked for?

That's what God's standard looks like in the thick of real life.

It's not squeaky clean. It's not Instagramable. But it's Christlike.

And in the end, that's what ethics is for – not to make you look morally superior, but to make you look more like Jesus.

Let's be honest: living by God's character is not a quick fix or a shiny life hack.

It's not something you master in a semester, like high school algebra (and even that felt sketchy by the time we got to imaginary numbers.) It's lifelong transformation, and some days you will feel like you're nailing it, while other days you'll wonder if you're just a very holy-looking train wreck, in progress,

Spoiler: you are not a wreck. You're a work.

You are God's workmanship, created in Christ Jesus for good works (Ephesians 2:10). That means you weren't just saved from sin; you were saved for something. And that "something" includes a life that reflects the holy, just, merciful, true, unchanging character of the God who called you.

Let that settle in for a second.

Your life is a portrait in progress – a living, breathing canvas that tells the truth about the Artist. And as long as you keep handing Him the brush, He'll keep shaping you.

But here's where it gets tricky: sometimes we confuse progress with perfection. We think if God is the standard and we're not meeting it yet, we must be failing.

That's not how grace works.

Grace doesn't say, "You should've been holy by now." Grace says, "You're not holy yet? Cool. Let's keep going."

God's standard doesn't crush us – it guides us.

It gives us a direction, a definition, a target that never moves even when we wobble. Because God is not just the goal – He's the power source.

He doesn't just show us the finish line. He runs with us.

And that's the good news buried in all this talk about ethics: you're not doing this alone.

You've got the Spirit of God inside you. You've got the living Word of God in your hands. You've got the example of Jesus ahead of you.

And let's not forget, you've got the people of God around you (yes, even the awkward ones).

Because ethics was never meant to be lived out in isolation. It's forged in community.

In fact, some of your most ethical moments will never be seen on a stage or posted in a caption.

They'll happen in private:

When you choose forgiveness even when bitterness feels more satisfying, when you close your laptop instead of giving in to that old temptation. When you admit you were wrong to your kids. When you return something, you could've kept. When you don't exaggerate the story to make yourself look better. When you sit with someone's pain instead of trying to fix it.

These are the moments that form your soul.

Not the big, flashy, impressive ones but the daily decisions to mirror the One you follow.

And let's be real, mirroring God is not something we just do. It's something we're empowered to do.

Let's bring it back to Scripture:

'According as he hath chosen us in him before the foundation of the world, that we should be holy and without blame before him in love."
Ephesians 1:4

That's not wishful thinking. That's God's intentional plan for you.

He chose you, not to be a slightly improved version of yourself, but to be holy, set apart, distinctly shaped by His character, blameless not because you're flawless, but because you've been forgiven and you're becoming.

And here's the beautiful twist: the more you grow in godly character, the more free you become.

Not rigid. Not robotic. Not morally constipated. Free.

Free from needing everyone's approval.

Free from the anxiety of trying to make your own rules.

Free from shame cycle and spiritual performance.

Free to walk in integrity because you know whose you are and who He is.

This is what happens when God's character becomes your compass, you stop chasing the world's definition of success, and you start living with clarity, peace, and quiet confidence in the Lord.

You stop aiming for perfection and start walking in faithfulness.

You realize that holiness is not about being squeaky clean on the outside, it's about being set apart on the inside.

And over time, that internal transformation spills out into everything.

Your speech. Your finances. Your parenting. Your friendships. Your dating choices. Your work ethics. Your conflict resolution. Your online presence. Even how you treat your enemies. (Yes. Even them.)

Because when God sets the standard, every part of your life gets reordered under His rule.

Not in a heavy-handed, "better follow the rules or else" kind of way. In a beautiful, liberating, "this is what we're made for" kind of way.

And let's be honest – this kind of life is weird.

You'll forgive when it doesn't make sense. You'll give when others hoard. You'll speak truth even when it costs you. You'll repent when you're wrong instead of doubling down. You'll bless people who mock you. You'll say no to things everyone else says yes to. You'll say yes to things others avoid because they're inconvenient.

But you won't be doing it to prove anything. You'll be doing it because you've been transformed.

You're no longer living for yourself. You're no longer the standard. God is.

And that's the best news in the world.

Because He's not just holy, He's good. He's not just just, He's merciful. He's not just true, He's patient. He's not just righteous, He's full of grace and truth, all at once.

You are not trying to mirror a dictator. You're mirroring a Father, one who knows your name, sees your struggle, and delights in every step you take toward Him.

Even the baby ones. Especially the baby ones.

So, as we close out this chapter, let's strip away the pressure and breathe in the invitation.

You don't have to carry the weight of being your own moral authority.

You don't have to figure it all out, fake it until you make it, or manufacture your own righteousness.

You get to trust God's character, lean into His Spirit, walk in His truth, and live out your calling one messy, grace-soaked day at a time.

And when you mess up? (Because yes, still.)

You confess. You repent. You receive mercy.

And when you get up and keep going – not because you're strong, but because your standard is strong enough to carry you.

Chapter 2:

The Authority of Scripture

(a.k.a. "Yes, God Really Did Say That – And He Meant It Too")

Let's talk about the Bible.

That leather-bound, coffee-stained bookmark-hoarding book sitting on your nightstand. Or possibly propping up a houseplant, depending on how your weeks been.

For Christians, the Bible isn't just a religious artifact, a source of inspirational quotes, or the reason your grandma won't get a tattoo. It is, and always has been, the foundational authority for what we believe, how we live, and how we understand the God we serve.

Or, at least, it's supposed to be.

But let's be honest. In a world of curated feeds, motivational reels, and hot-take theology served in 30-second bursts, the idea that an ancient book, especially one written in King James English, should tell you how to live? That can sound...quaint. Maybe even oppressive. Or, at best, wildly outdated.

I mean, how can a 2,000-year-old compilation of scrolls and letters have any authority over my digital-age life? What does "thou shalt not" have to say to my Google calendar, my group chat, or my ongoing addiction to overthinking every conversation I've ever had since middle school?

The answer?

Everything.

Because Scripture isn't just old. It's alive.

It doesn't just speak to the past, it speaks with the voice of the God who made you, knows you, and is still writing your story.

And if we're going to talk Christian ethics – how to live, how to think, how to love, how to work, how to navigate a world that's morally upside-down, we have to start with the question: Who gets the final say?

Spoiler: it's not your feelings. It's not your favorite influencer. It's not a panel of progressive opinions or a nostalgic return to "the good old days."

It's the Word of God.

And yes – we're talking about the King James Version here.

Now, before you panic and run for your "easier to read" translation, hear me out. The KJV isn't about confusing people with "thee" and "thou." It's about preserving the richness, reverence, and depth of Scripture in a form that's stood the test of time.

When you open the KJV, you're not reading a motivational pamphlet. You're entering a cathedral. You're stepping into sacred ground.

This isn't just ancient literature. It's breathed by God. (2 Timothy 3:16). Inspired. Inerrant. Authoritative.

Not just helpful. Holy.

That means the Bible isn't optional for Christians. It's essential.

It's not background noise for your life – it's the foundation beneath it.

And when it comes to ethics? The Bible doesn't just give you random advice, it reveals the very mind of God.

The laws, the principles, the parables, the prophecies, the poetry, the commands, the red letters, they all work together to show you what righteousness looks like in real life.

Without Scripture, Christian ethics becomes guesswork. It becomes a choose-your-own-adventure, morality based on vibes and opinions.

But with Scripture?

You get clarity.

You get conviction.

You get truth that transcends time.

So why does it matter that the Bible has authority?

Why can't we just treat it like a spiritual buffet, grab the Psalms for comfort, skip Leviticus like kale salad, sprinkle in a few red letters of Jesus, and call it a balanced diet?

Because Scripture was never meant to be consumed selectively. It was meant to be submitted to.

Yes, I know. "Submission" isn't exactly trending on TikTok. It sounds a little intense. A little outdated. Maybe even oppressive. But before you go full eye-roll, let's unpack it.

Submission to Scripture doesn't mean turning off your brain and blindly following ancient rules. It means recognizing that God knows more than you.

Shocking, I know.

It means trusting that the One who designed the universe, understands your wiring, sees the future, and knit you together in your mother's womb, might – just might – have a better grasp on truth than your morning mood or your favorite podcast.

And here's the thing: everybody submits to something.

We all have a final authority. For some, it's their emotions. For others, it's culture. For many, its just...whatever sounds right in the moment.

But for the Christian? The Bible is the plumb line.

It's the anchor in a world of drifting opinions. The true north in a world full of spinning compasses. The light in a very, very foggy forest.

"Thy word is a lamp unto my feet, and a light unto my path." Psalm 119:105

That verse doesn't say "a spotlight that shows the whole journey." It says lamp. Meaning? The Bible might not tell you everything about your future career, your dating life, or whether you should text them back…But it will tell you how to walk.

Ethically. Honestly. Righteously. Like someone who doesn't just know about God, but lives under His rule.

That's what authority means. Not, "God is bossy." But, "God is King." And His Word is not just a guide – it's law.

And yes, I said the "L" word. Law.

The kind of law that tells you what's right not because it's convenient, but because it reflects the unchanging nature of God.

The kind of law that limits your behaviour not to punish you, but to preserve you.

See, Scripture doesn't just keep you in check – it keeps you aligned.

Like a chiropractor for your soul. Slightly painful at first, but oh-so-necessary.

Because if your ethics are out of alignment with God's Word, it's only a matter of time before something starts to hurt – your relationships, your conscience, your witness, or all three.

Here's where the KJV angle matters. Not just because it poetic or traditional (though both are true), but because the translation is rooted in reverence.

Every "thou" and "thine" isn't just an old-timey flex. It reminds us that we're reading something holy, not casual.

This isn't divine suggestion – it's divine revelation.

God is not hoping to be quoted. He's expecting to be obeyed.

And yes, there's grace. We'll get to that. But let's not skip over the weight of what Scripture actually is:

It is **the breath of God** (2 Timothy 3:16).

It is **forever settled in heaven** (Psalm 119:89).

It is **pure, tried, and flawless** (Psalm 12:6).

And it will **outlast heaven and earth** (Matthew 24:35).

That means when the world changes its mind again – and it will – you won't be shaken. Because your life is built on something eternal.

And don't miss this: when you live under the authority of Scripture, you're not shrinking your life, you're anchoring it.

You're becoming someone who can't be manipulated by every cultural wave. Someone who doesn't cave when compromise looks easier. Someone who doesn't trade conviction for comfort.

You're becoming immovable in the best way.

Not hard-hearted. Not inflexible. But deeply rooted in the truth of a God who speaks and still means what He says.

Even when it's hard. Even when it's costly. Even when it doesn't feel affirming.

Because the authority of Scripture isn't about feeling good – it's about being formed.

And God is more committed to your formation than your comfort.

Which is exactly what we'll talk about next: what happens when Scripture confronts us – and why that's actually a gift.

Ready to keep going?

Let's talk about one of the least comfortable truths about Scripture:

Sometimes – it hurts.

I don't mean "I stubbed my toe on a Bible" hurt. I mean soul-deep, ego-deflating, conviction-stabbing, "Oh wow, I was today years old when I realized I was wrong" kind of hurt.

And honestly? That's a good thing.

Because if Scripture never challenges you, you're probably not reading it, you're not using it.

See, the Bible isn't a weapon you wield at others to win arguments. It's a mirror that reveals your own heart first.

And let's be clear: it's a brutally honest mirror. Not the kind with good lighting and filters. The kind you find in dressing rooms with overhead lights and no mercy.

But that's what makes it powerful.

"For the word of God is quick, and powerful, and sharper than any twoedged sword, piercing to the dividing asunder of soul and spirit...and is a discerner of the thoughts and intents of the heart." Hebrews 4:12

The Bible doesn't just tell you what you did. It tells you why you did it.

It cuts through the fluff, the self-justification, the "I meant well's" and "it's not that bad's" and reveals your motives. Your priorities. Your deep-down, behind-the-scenes heart stuff.

And no, it's not always comfortable. But it's always good.

Because God's goal isn't to shame you, it's to transform you.

He doesn't expose to embarrass. He exposes to heal.

Kind of like a surgeon. If a doctor cuts you open, you're not suing him, you're thanking him for removing what was killing you.

That's what Scripture does. It gets in deep. It messes with your categories. It calls out your quiet sins, not just your public ones. It confronts your bitterness, your pride, your laziness, your excuses, your passive-aggression, your control issues – yes, even your need to correct people on the internet.

It reads you while you're reading it.

And that's the point.

Because you don't grow in holiness by reading only what agrees with you. You grow by letting God's Word disagree with you and then obeying anyway.

Yes, even when it offends you.

Especially when it offends you.

Because if the Bible never offends you, you're not following God, you're following a you-shaped echo chamber.

Here's the thing: our culture has trained us to believe that offense = harm. That if something makes you uncomfortable, it must be wrong or unsafe.

But Scripture lovingly says, "Actually, discomfort might be the first sign of growth."

It's like exercise for your soul. No one enjoys leg day. But you'll be glad for the strength it produces. Same with Scripture. Sometimes it leaves you sore – but more solid.

And this is where authority comes back into the picture.

Because when the Bible confronts your pride, you have two options:

Submit to it.

Reinterpret it until it says what you wanted it to say.

Guess which one leads to transformation?

(Yeah. The hard one.)

We've all seen people twist Scripture. Snipping verses out of context like theological paper dolls.

Using the Bible like a meme generator – only pulling out what reinforces their existing views.

But if the Word of God is truly authoritative, we don't get to be its editors. We are its students.

We sit under it, not over it. We align to it, not the other way around.

And listen, you don't have to like everything the Bible says at first. God isn't threatened by your emotional reactions. But you do have to wrestle with it.

And wrestling is good.

In fact, Jacob wrestled with God all night and came out of it blessed and limping, which honestly might be the perfect metaphor for Christian ethics.

You walk away changed. A little humbled. Maybe a little sore. But marked by God.

That's what happens when you let Scripture confront you. You learn that truth isn't always gentle, but it's always loving. You learn that conviction isn't cruelty, it's care. You learn that God doesn't expose you to ruin you, He reveals so He can rebuild.

So, when you feel the sting of a verse that hits a little too close to home? Don't scroll past it.

Sit with it.

Pray through it.

Ask the Spirit, "What are You showing me here? What do You want to change?"

And then, take a step.

No matter how small. No matter how slow.

That's ethics in action: saying yes to God even when it costs you something.

Because let's face it, there will always be an easier option. A softer path. A less convicting route. But nothing will make you more like Jesus than trusting that His Word is not only right, it's best.

And that's how authority becomes freedom.

Not by skipping the hard parts. But by walking through them, holding onto the God who knows exactly what He's doing.

So far, we've talked about how Scripture guides us, confronts us, and corrects us. But now let's go a step deeper.

Because the Bible doesn't just tell you what to do, it tells you who you are.

And let me tell you – this matters. A lot.

Because we live in a world that's having a full-blown identity crisis.

Everywhere you turn, people are scrambling to figure out who they are, what they're worth, and where they belong. And they're looking in all the usual places:

Personality tests.

Enneagram numbers

Instagram bios.

Career titles.

Zodiac signs.

Spotify playlists.

("I'm a type 4 introvert with a Scorpion moon and a side of worship anthems and breakup songs." Cool. But...now what?)

None of these things are evil. Some are even helpful in moderation. But none of them can answer the deepest questions of your soul.

Questions like:

Who made me?

What was I made for?

What defines my worth?

What's my purpose?

Can I be loved even when I messed up?

Only one book answers all those with eternal clarity.

And spoiler: it's not your birth chart.

It's the Word of God.

The Bible doesn't give you a curated identity, it gives you a created one.

You're not a random accident. You're not a personality score. You're not a sum of your traumas or triumphs. You are:

Created in the image of God (Genesis 1:27)

Knit together in your mother's womb (Psalm 139:13)

Fearfully and wonderfully made (Psalm 139:14)

Known, chosen, and called (Jeremiah 1:5, Ephesians 1:4)

Redeemed through the blood of Jesus (Ephesians 1:7)

A new creation (2 Corinthians 5:17)

A temple of the Holy Spirit (1 Corinthians 6:19)

A citizen of heaven (Philippians 3:20)

God's workmanship, created for good works (Ephesians 2:10)

That's who you are.

And no trend, trauma, achievement, or failure can redefine it.

Not your family history. Not your past mistakes. Not your current doubts. Not your follower count. Not even your feelings.

Especially not your feelings.

Because here's the thing, your feelings are real, but they're not always true.

That's why you need something outside of yourself to define you. Something stable. Something eternal. Something that doesn't change with your moods or your mistakes.

You need Scripture.

The Bible is the only mirror that tells the truth. Not just about what's wrong, but about what's right in Christ.

And when you know who you are in Him, ethics stops being about behaviour management, it becomes an identity response.

You don't forget to impress God; you forgive because you've been forgiven. You don't live holy to earn love, you live holy because you are loved. You don't resist sin to prove something; you resist because sin no longer owns you.

You start to see that obedience isn't a cage, it's evidence.

Evidence that something real has changed inside you. Evidence that you are no longer who you used to be. And let me say this plainly: you don't have to keep performing to prove you're worthy.

Jesus already did that for you.

And His Word confirms it over and over.

When you fail?

Romans 8:1 – "There is therefore now no condemnation to them which are in Christ Jesus..."

When you doubt your purpose?

Jeremiah 29:11 – "For I know the thoughts that I think toward you, saith the Lord..."

When you feel forgotten?

Isaiah 49:15 – "Yet will I not forget thee."

When the shame creeps in?

Micah 7:19 – "He will subdue our iniquities; and thou wilt cast all their sins into the depths of the sea."

When the enemy whispers, "You'll never change?"

2 Corinthians 3:18 – "We all...are changed into the same image from glory to glory..."

God's Word doesn't just tell you what to do. It tells you that you are not alone, not abandoned, and not unredeemable.

You are God's.

And that identity changes how you live.

It gives you courage when obedience feels costly. It gives you clarity when the world is shouting a thousand definitions. It gives you compassion for others, because if God rescued you, He can rescue anyone.

So no, Christian ethics isn't about behaviour modification. It's about identity revelation.

You live differently because you know who you are. You know Whose voice has the authority to define you. And you trust that if God says something in His Word, it's not just true. It's true about you.

That's the power of Scripture.

It doesn't just teach you – it transforms.

It doesn't just inform – it invites.

It doesn't just correct – it confirms who you are in Christ.

And when you live out that identity? You become a person of conviction, peace, and purpose.

Not because you figured it all out, but because you finally stopped trying to be your own god, and let God's Word have the final say.

By now, we've established that Scripture is powerful, personal, convicting, and identity shaping. But here's another beautiful truth we can't miss:

Scripture trains you.

Yes, trains. Like a coach. Like a personal trainer, but instead of yelling "One more rep!" it's saying, "Here's how you live righteously even when you're tired, frustrated, and tempted to tell someone off in traffic."

The Bible is not just a list of moral dos and don'ts. It's a full-on formation tool.

"All scripture is given by inspiration of God, and is profitable for doctrine, for reproof, for correction, for instruction in righteousness," 2 Timothy 3:16

Let's break that down:

Doctrine – What is true.

Reproof – What's wrong.

Correction – How to get back on track.

Instruction in righteousness – How to stay on track.

It's a four-part discipleship system packed into one verse. And the cool part? It applies to literally every area of your life.

Scripture is not just profitable when you're doing a quiet time and sipping peppermint tea. It's profitable when life gets messy.

Like:

When you're making a major life decision and need wisdom.

When you're discouraged and need to be reminded of your identity.

When you're drifting into apathy and need a wake-up call.

When your integrity is tested, and everyone's cutting corners but you.

When you're tempted to justify sin because, "God knows your heart," (He does...and that's not always the comfort we think it is.)

Scripture doesn't just keep you moral. It keeps you sharp.

It teaches you how to:

Speak the truth in love.

Stay humble when praised.

Stay steady when criticized.

Keep going when you're exhausted.

Rest when the world tells you to hustle.

Pray when you'd rather post about it.

Hold a boundary without becoming bitter.

Apologize without shifting blame.

Wait on God without jumping ahead.

And here's the miracle: the more you read the Word, the more the Word reads you.

It gets into your instincts. It shapes your reactions. It builds spiritual reflexes.

One day, you'll look back and realize that you responded with patience in a situation that would've made you rage two years ago. And you'll go, "Wait. Where did that come from?"

Answer: it came from being trained.

You've been quietly, steadily formed by God's Word.

Because that's what training is, small acts of faithfulness, over time, that produces quiet strength. And let me tell you, this world needs people with quiet strength. It doesn't need more hot takes or flashy virtue-signaling. It needs people who have let Scripture work them over in the hidden places. People whose obedience isn't performative but anchored.

People who won't fold when culture shifts, who won't ghost when things get uncomfortable, who won't edit the Bible to make it trend better.

People who are the same behind closed doors as they are in public, because their lives are governed by the Word of God, not the applause of man.

That's the kind of person Scripture produces.

And get this; Scripture doesn't just train you for life, it trains you for every good work (see the very next verse, 2 Timothy 3:17).

That means the Bible is not just useful for church stuff. It's useful for; parenting, running a business, leading a team, serving in your community, making art, building healthy boundaries, writing emails without passive-aggression, loving difficult people without enabling their nonsense.

Why? Because Scripture doesn't just shape your morals, it shapes your motives. It doesn't just clean up your act, it aligns your heart with God's. It teaches you to stop asking, "What can I get away with?" and start asking, "What would honor the Lord in this moment?"

That's a different kind of Christian. That's a different kind of life. It's not always glamorous. It's definitely not always easy. But it's real.

And it's rare.

Because here's the truth, you will be shaped by something.

Culture will shape you. Pain will shape you. Trauma will shape you. Netflix algorithms will shape you. Bitterness will shape you.

Unless...you let Scripture do it first. Unless you make a daily, sometimes boring, wildly powerful decision to come under the authority of the Word, again and again.

That's what it means to be a disciple.

You're not just following Jesus in theory. You're following Him in your actual everyday decisions. You're letting the Word coach you, correct you, confront you, and comfort you. You're saying, "I trust this more than I trust myself."

That's not weakness. That's maturity.

And that's how you go from an inconsistent, emotionally reactive, part-time believer...to a fruit-bearing, steady-hearted, truth-walking ambassador of Christ.

Not overnight. Not perfectly. But truly. Because the Word of God isn't just a book. It's a lifeline.

And the more you grab hold of it, the more it will shape everything about you, from how you handle money, to how you treat your enemies, to how you interpret your suffering.

If you've been alive for more than seven minutes, you've probably noticed we live in a world where everything is up for debate.

Everything.

Truth is relative. Morality is flexible. Everyone's "truth" is sacred...as long as it doesn't contradict someone else's.

It's like we're all walking around with DIY moral compasses, but instead of pointing north, they are just pointing toward whatever we're currently feeling.

And then we wonder why everyone's lost.

Enter, the authority of Scripture.

Because when the fog rolls in, when the ethical landscape gets murky, when the culture says one thing and your instincts say another, when your feelings start arguing with your faith, you need more than a good guess.

You need clarity.

And clarity only comes from something more stable than you. That's what makes the Bible so refreshing, and so offensive. Because the Bible doesn't change when society does. It doesn't upgrade its values with the times. It doesn't repackage truth to make it more palatable. It doesn't care if it's commandments trend on X or get canceled in your group chat.

The Word of God is eternally clear, even when we wish it weren't. And thank God for that. Because moral clarity isn't a burden. It's a lifeline.

It frees you from the exhausting treadmill of self-made ethics. It rescues you from the swamp of moral relativism. It gives you a solid "yes" and "no" in a world addicted to "maybe."

Let's get specific.

Culture says, "You do you."
Scripture says, "Deny yourself, take up your cross, and follow Jesus." (Matthew 16:24, Mark 8:34, Luke 9:23)

Culture says, "Love is love."
Scripture says, "Love rejoices in the truth." (1 Corinthian 13:6)

Culture says, "Live your truth."
Scripture says, "I am the way, the truth, and the life." (John 14:6)

Culture says, "You only live once."
Scripture says, "It is appointed unto men once to die, but after this the judgement." (Hebrews 9:27)

These are not small differences.

They are radically different visions of reality. One is built on ever-shifting sand. The other is grounded in the eternal Word of God.

And here's the best part, Scripture doesn't just give clarity in the big cultural issues. It gives clarity in the personal, awkward, every day messes too.

When you're deciding whether to confront a friend or let it go. When you're wrestling with guilt but aren't sure if it's conviction or condemnation. When you're dating someone and the lines are starting to blur. When you're not sure how to respond to a crisis or injustice. When you feel the pull of pride and want to know if it's boldness or bravado. When you're trying to parent without losing your mind. (Bless you.)

In those moments, clarity is gold.

And the Bible offers it, every time. It won't always give you a step-by-step plan. But it will always show you the heart of God. And that's often the clarity you need.

Because God's heart is steady. His Word is sure. And when you're confused, you don't need a sign, you need Scripture.

This is why Christians for centuries have run to the Word when everything else falls apart.

When nations fall. When families break. When friendships crack. When injustice surges. When fear creeps in. When apathy sets in.

The Word of God is still there. Still true. Still clear. Still speaking.

"The entrance of thy words giveth light; it giveth understanding unto the simple." Psalm 119:130

You don't need to be a scholar. You don't need to have it all figured out. You just need to open the Word and let the light in.

Because here's the real danger in a blurry world. If you don't let Scripture define what's true, something else will.

And that "something else" will often sound nice. It will sound spiritual. It might even use some Bible-ish language. But it will be off.

Just enough to twist the truth. Just enough to feel good while quietly pulling you off course. That's how deception works. It doesn't come dressed in horns and red flags. It comes wearing a Christian T-shirt and quoting half a verse.

That's why clarity matters. That's why authority matters.

Because if God's Word has authority in your life, you won't fall for every emotionally charged, well-designed lie that comes your way.

You'll be able to test the spirits. You'll be able to spot the counterfeit. You'll be able to stay steady in chaos.

Because you're not living off vibes. You're living off truth. And truth isn't a concept. It's a person.

"Sanctify them through thy truth; thy word is truth." John 17:17

Jesus prayed that over His disciples. Over you.

He knew we'd be walking through a world where everything's foggy, and He gave us a blazing light: His Word.

Don't ignore it. Don't dilute it. Don't let culture rewrite it. Just read it. Trust it. Obey it. Let it be the voice that rises above every other voice in your life.

Because when you live under the authority of Scripture, clarity isn't something you have to strive for, it's something you stand in.

Let's be honest, clinging to the authority of Scripture isn't exactly trending. Some people see it as rigid, outdated, or even dangerous. Like saying you still burn CDs or churn your own butter. But we don't hold fast to God's Word because we're nostalgic. We hold to it because it's the only thing that stands when everything else falls apart.

The world doesn't just disagree with Scripture anymore; it actively resists it. And that puts every follower of Christ in a tension-filled position.

We each have a choice to make, stand on what God has said, or slide into whatever feels safer, softer, more socially acceptable.

Following Jesus isn't just about nodding in agreement on Sundays. It's about actual obedience when it's inconvenient on Mondays, in meetings, in traffic, and in complicated conversations. Especially when doing so costs something.

Taking Scripture seriously may stretch your friendships, limit career paths, or challenge your comfort. It might mean losing people's approval. But in exchange, you walk in the approval of God.

And that trade is worth everything.

Obedience may not be fashionable, but it's powerful. Rare, yes, but powerful. The people God often uses most aren't the loudest or flashiest. They're simply the ones who stay rooted.

"He shall be like a tree planted by the rivers of water, that bringeth forth his fruit in his season..." Psalm 1:3

Trees don't chase trends. They don't panic in bad weather. They just stay planted and let their roots do the work. That's what Scripture can do in your life, it grounds you. It teaches you to be steady, even when culture demands flexibility or your fears tell you to hide.

When rooted in the Word, you're not just morally informed – you're morally equipped. The Bible gives more than clarity. It gives courage.

And that's exactly what's needed when you're the only one who doesn't laugh at the joke, join in the gossip, or compromise for comfort.

Courage doesn't have to be loud. Often, it looks like quiet refusal, a steady commitment not to bend when everything around you is shifting.

Scripture helps form that kind of strength. The more it fills your heart, the less space there is for compromise to grow. Over time, it shapes your instincts. You begin to think differently, speak with more care, and respond with grace and wisdom instead of reaction.

When your ethics are built in private with God, you won't be scrambling to figure them out in public. You've already made the decision, now you just walk in it.

That's how Jesus did it.

In the wilderness, when Satan tempted Him, He didn't bargain or overthink. He simply replied, "It is written." Again, and again. Not with a new revelation, but with Scripture He already had internalized. The Son of God used the written Word to defeat lies, and we're not stronger than Him.

Temptation isn't defeated by raw willpower. It's defeated by truth that's already taken root.

And here's where the King James Version still holds a unique weight. Its formality demands pause, reflection, reverence. It's not about nostalgia; it's about slowing down enough to actually let the truth sink in.

Understanding the gist isn't the goal. Transformation is.

You may not always feel inspired during your Bible reading. You won't always have emotional breakthroughs. But those words are still working, forming, growing something within you that will stand the test when it comes.

Over time, that quiet formation produces someone others begin to trust. Not because you're impressive, but because you're consistent, you're a reference point.

And that's the other gift Scripture gives, discernment.

You begin to notice what others miss. You can sense the off-notes in something that sounds spiritual but lacks substance. The Word becomes your turning fork. Everything else is measured against it.

You don't have to guess. You don't need to Google whether something is right. You already know how to test it.

A catchy quote, a viral post, even a sermon, if it doesn't align with the voice of Scripture, it's not worth building your life on.

And when it doesn't line up?

You don't have to start a crusade. You simply walk the other way. No drama. No rudeness. Just a quiet resolve. And in today's noisy world, that kind of clarity is compelling.

The world isn't desperate for more spiritually trendy voices. It's starving for people who are steady. People whose lives are shaped by truth that doesn't wobble with the news cycle or the latest controversy.

What's needed most is a generation of believers who walk in humility and conviction, speak truth with compassion, and live with the kind of calm that only eternity can provide.

That's what Scripture does.

It grounds. It's steady. It gives strength in a world built on sand.

And sometimes, the most radical thing you can do is keep obeying God, not loudly, but faithfully. Not for applause, but because He said so. That's not weakness. That's spiritual maturity.

It doesn't happen overnight. It happens one obedient choice at a time.

One verse, one response, one act of faith when no one's watching.

Let's bring this home.

We've explored the power of Scripture, how it teaches, confronts, shapes, and steadies us. But maybe the biggest takeaway is this: if the Bible is truly authoritative, it changes not just how you think, but how you live.

Not in a performative, "look how holy I am" way. But in a quiet, real-life way. The kind of transformation that shows up in everyday decisions. In how you speak, how you forgive, how you spend your money, and how you respond when no one's watching.

This isn't about striving for perfection or earning spiritual gold stars. It's about living under the gentle, unshakable guidance of God's Word. And that kind of life takes shape slowly – verse by verse, decision by decision.

Some day, reading Scripture will feel rich and deep. Other days it'll feel dry or difficult. That's okay. You're not chasing a feeling; you're following a faithful God. One who speaks through His Word even when your coffee's cold and your mind's distracted.

The goal isn't to master the Bible. It's to let the Bible master you.

Over time, something shifts. You begin to recognize when your thoughts are drifting off course. You catch yourself before reacting in pride. You choose love over convenience, truth over comfort, prayer over panic.

You become more stable. Not perfect. But grounded.

And in a world that is anything but grounded, that's a powerful testimony.

People notice. They may not be able to explain it, but they'll sense something different. The peace. The conviction. The quiet strength. It speaks louder than any sermon you could preach.

That's the beauty of a life formed by Scripture. It doesn't need a spotlight to make an impact. It simply reflects God's wisdom, His kindness, His consistency.

So, what now?

Keep showing up. Keep reading. Keep letting the Word press into the places that need it. The messy places. The wounded ones. The prideful ones too.

Let it remind you who you are and whose you are. Let it speak louder than your fears and more clearly than your doubts. Let it challenge your assumptions and confirm your calling.

And when you're unsure about the world, about your next step, about your place in it all – open the Bible again. The same God who breathed stars into existence also breathed out this Book. He knew you'd need something unchanging. Something you could trust when everything else started to unravel.

His Word is enough.

Not just for Sunday school answers, but for hospital rooms and hard conversations. For interviews and midnight prayers. For raising kids, confessing sin, rebuilding trust, and remembering grace.

You don't need to reinvent truth. You just need to return to it.

Again, and again. Gritty faithfulness, not flashy perfection.

Because His Word, these pages, this voice, won't fail you. It never has.

And if you're willing to stake your life on it, you'll find it's more than ancient wisdom or moral advice. It's a life-giving, heart-transforming, eternity-pointing truth.

Unchanging. Undeniable. Unapologetically holy.

Chapter 3:

"The Moral Law:
Old Testament Foundations"

Let's get one thing straight, nobody throws a party over the phrase "moral law," It's not exactly a conversation starter. In fact, if you want a group of modern Christians to awkwardly reach for their phones or disappear into their coffee mugs, just say, "Let's talk about the Ten Commandments."

We treat God's law like that old relative we respect, but don't quite know what to do with. We know it's important, we've seen it hanging in courtrooms, crocheted on wall hanging, or quoted in epic Charlton Heston tones. But when it comes to real-life relevance? That's where things get a little murky.

Some folks act like the Old Testament moral law is the ancient, grumpy version of God's Word. Strict, hard-edged, and a little out of touch. As if Jesus showed up and said, "Okay, everyone chill out. Let's forget that whole 'thou shalt not' stuff and just vibe." But spoiler alert: He didn't.

Jesus didn't come to erase the law. He came to fulfill it.

That means the law isn't expired, it's foundational.

And before you run for the hills, let me say this. Understanding the moral law isn't about becoming a dusty theologian or a rules-obsessed robot.

It's about discovering the heart of a holy God who actually cares about how we live, how we treat each other, and how we reflect His character.

Because here's the deal. God didn't give Israel the law to kill their joy. He gave it to shape their identity.

These weren't arbitrary commands tossed from the sky like divine post-it notes. They were boundary lines that carved out a people who would look different than the world around them. While other nations were bowing to statues, sacrificing children, and inventing creative ways to sin, God was forming a people marked by justice, mercy, and order.

The law wasn't a burden. It was a gift.

Think of it like this. When a builder starts a house, they don't wing it. They use a blueprint. Structure matters. Foundation matters. Otherwise, you get a crooked house that looks fine until the wind picks up, and then everything falls apart.

That's what the moral law is. It's the blueprint of righteousness. And the Ten Commandments? They're the opening page.

Now, I know what some might be thinking, "But isn't that just for Israel?

We're under grace now." Yes, we are under grace, gloriously, undeservedly so. But grace doesn't nullify truth; it illuminates it.

When Jesus was asked which commandment was the greatest, He didn't cancel the Ten. He summarized them.

"Thou shalt love the Lord thy God with all thy heart, and with all thy soul, and with all thy mind...And the second is like unto it, Thou shalt love thy neighbour as thyself." Matthew 22:37, 39

Love God. Love others. That's the heartbeat of the law. The Ten Commandments? They simply give that love some teeth.

Let's be honest, "love your neighbour" is easy to say, but it's the law that helps us figure out what that actually looks like. It's not loving to lie, steal, or commit adultery. It's not loving to dishonor parents or bear false witness. So, the law isn't fighting against love; it's protecting it.

In other words, the law isn't legalism, it's love in action.

And just in case you've forgotten what those Ten Commandments actually are (no shame, it's not like we recite them at brunch), here's a quick refresher, straight from Exodus 20:

1. No other gods before Me.
2. No idols.
3. Don't misuse God's name.
4. Keep the Sabbath holy.
5. Honor your father and mother.
6. Don't murder.
7. Don't commit adultery.
8. Don't steal.
9. Don't lie about your neighbor.
10. Don't covet what isn't yours.

Notice something? The first four focus on our relationship with God. The last six focus on our relationship with people. That's not accidental, it's divine design. Love God. Love others. Two tablets, one heart.

And these commandments? They aren't just religious relics. They still expose our hearts.

We may not bow to golden calves, but we sure do worship money, status, and our own Instagram feeds.

We may not commit physical murder, but we'll assassinate someone's character in a heartbeat, with sarcasm, gossip, or a pointed passive-aggressive meme.

We may not carve idols from stone, but we've made self-expression into its religion.

The law still reveals how far we fall short. And that's part of its purpose, to diagnose the soul. It's like a spiritual X-ray vision. It shows us what's broken. And while it can't fix us (that's where grace and the cross come in), it does what only truth can; it points us to the healer.

Now, if you've ever read through Leviticus and felt like you accidentally opened God's kitchen manual ("don't boil a goat in its mother's milk" – um, noted), you might wonder how to separate moral law from ceremonial or civil law.

Great question. Here's a breakdown:

Ceremonial laws dealt with worship practices (sacrifices, priesthood, temple rules).

Civil laws were specific to Israel as a theocratic nation (property rights, community discipline).

Moral laws reflect God's unchanging character and applied universally.

Ceremonial laws were fulfilled in Christ (that's why we don't bring doves to church). Civil laws governed ancient Israel's society. But moral law? They still reveal what God loves and what He calls sin.

The Ten Commandments are moral laws. Eternal, unchanging, and still completely relevant – even if the font on your Bible app changes every month.

So, when we talk about Christian ethics, we're not making it up as we go. We're building on something ancient, sacred, and solid.

That's why this foundation matters. Because if we don't understand the moral law, we end up with ethics built on vibes and emotions.

And feelings make terrible moral compasses. Today's impulse becomes tomorrow's regret.

But God's moral law? It doesn't shift with the culture. It doesn't cave under pressure. It stands tall – like a mountain that's seen storms come and go, still unmoved.

And if we'll stop treating it like spiritual fine print and start viewing it as a guide for thriving, not just surviving, we might just rediscover the beauty of living under the authority of a good, holy God.

We left off with the Ten Commandments standing like a mountain, immovable, timeless, and honestly, kind of intimidating. But now it's time to zoom in and see how this moral law actually intersects with our lives. Not in abstract, theological headspace, but in the day-to-day decisions that define who we're becoming.

Because here's the thing, most of us aren't out here plotting murder or building shrines to Baal. But that doesn't mean we're nailing it morally. In fact, the genius of the moral law is that it keeps peeling layers of the heart. It won't let you off the hook with surface-level obedience. It goes deeper.

Let's take a few examples.

Commandment #1: No other gods before Me.

Now, you may not have a pagan altar in your living room (if you do, this chapter just got real urgent), but that doesn't mean this one's irrelevant. What owns your loyalty? What gets your best energy, your deepest trust, your unquestioned devotion? For some, it's money. For others, it's control, achievement, romance, or even ministry itself.

Idolatry today doesn't usually wear a name tag. It just quietly demands that we rearrange our lives around something other than God.

Commandment #2: Don't misuse the name of the Lord.

This isn't just about yelling "Oh my God!" in traffic (although words do matter). It's also about attaching God's name to things He never endorsed; like using spirituality to manipulate people, justify sin, or cover for selfish ambition.

To take His name in vain is to use it lightly, selfishly, or falsely. That's sobering.

Commandment #4: Do not murder.

Okay, this feels safe. Most of us can confidently say we haven't murdered anyone. Gold star, right? But then Jesus ruins our comfort in Matthew 5 and says if you harbor anger or insult someone without cause, you're walking in the same spiritual path. Great. Now that passive-aggressive email is looking a little darker. Murder isn't just an act, it's an attitude.

And that's the point.

The moral law digs beneath behaviour to get to character. It's not just about what you do with your hands, it's about what's growing in your heart. It's like God saying, "I'm not after robotic compliance. I'm after people who reflect My heart."

Let's talk about that for a minute. Because some Christians still think of the Old Testament God as the grumpy one, and the New Testament Jesus as the chill one. As if they're playing theological good cop/bad cop.

But the God who gave the law is the same God who hung on a cross.

The same mercy. The same holiness. The same love.

He didn't mellow out in the NT. He fulfilled what we couldn't, then handed us His Spirit so we could finally walk in what the law pointed toward all along.

Because the law was never the problem. The law is holy, good, and right.

We are the ones who missed the mark.

Which is why Paul says:

"Wherefore the law is holy, and the commandment holy, and just, and good."
Romans 7:12

The law reveals the standard. Grace provides the strength.

When we understand the law rightly, we stop seeing it as an obstacle to grace and start seeing it as the backdrop that makes grace stunning.

Imagine going to a jeweler and looking at a diamond laid on top of a clear glass countertop. It might sparkle, but it won't strike you. Now imagine that same diamond displayed against black velvet. Suddenly, the clarity and brilliance jump out.

That's what the moral law does, it's the velvet backdrop that reveals the brilliance of grace. You can't appreciate salvation until you know what you've been saved from.

But it doesn't stop there. The moral laws aren't just there to convict, it's there to guide. It gives us a target. A framework for living with wisdom, holiness, and love. A way to reflect God's character in real life.

Let me put it another way: the law is like a mirror. It shows you where your hair's doing something weird, or when spinach got stuck in your teeth. But the mirror can't fix the problem. It just reveals it. That's where grace comes in with the toothbrush and the comb (spiritually speaking).

Still, without the mirror, you wouldn't even know what needed attention.

That's why we don't discard the law. We need it. Not for salvation, but for sanctification. It helps us see clearly. It calls us higher. It reminds us of the holiness of the God we serve.

And honestly? The world is starving for this kind of clarity.

We live in a culture allergic to boundaries. Everyone wants to be their own moral authority. But that leads to chaos, not freedom. When "right" and "wrong" become personalized suggestions, we all end up more confused, more exhausted, and less human.

God's law, on the other hand, is a stabilizer.

It tells us that truth isn't fluid, that holiness isn't optional, and that love isn't blind approval; it's anchored in reality. The law doesn't shackle us. It steers us.

It also keeps us from self-deception. You know the drill: "Well, I'm basically a good person," or "God knows my heart," or "At least I'm not like that guy." But when you hold yourself up against the Ten Commandments – not as a checklist, but as a heart check – you quickly realize: we all fall short.

And that's exactly the point.

The law shows us our need. Not so we wallow in guilt, but so we run to grace.

God never expected Israel to perfectly keep the law on their own strength. He wanted them to walk in obedience through dependence – leaning on Him, trusting Him, repenting when they failed.

Same goes for us.

We don't keep the law to earn love. We follow it because we're loved, and we want to live like it.

You'd think that once we realize the law shows us our sin, we'd embrace it with open arms. "Ah yes, thank you for revealing how off-track I am!" But if we're being honest, our natural reaction is a bit more...allergic. Conviction doesn't feel cozy. It pokes at the parts of us we'd rather ignore.

That's why some Christians prefer to live in "grace-only" mode, as if acknowledging the moral law somehow cancels out mercy. But grace that never confronts sin isn't biblical grace. That's just permission with a smiley face.

Grace is not the opposite of law – it's the power to walk in what the law calls good.

And if we lose sight of the law, we lose sight of what good even is.

Think about it. The law doesn't just forbid evil; it reveals what matters to God. It protects the vulnerable. It honors truth. It establishes order. It reflects a God who is just, holy, and wise.

So, when we ignore or dilute the moral law, we're not just avoiding rules, we're distancing ourselves from His character.

For example, God didn't say "don't steal" because He's stingy. He said it because He values trust, integrity, and respect for what belongs to others.

He didn't say "don't lie" because He's obsessed with technical accuracy. He said it because He is truth. And when we lie, we break something sacred – relationships, reputations, even our own integrity.

He didn't say "don't covet" because He's against ambition.

He said it because when we're consumed by comparison, we stop being present. We lose gratitude. We forget His provision.

That's the key – every command points us to what God values.

And when we obey out of love, those values start to take root in us. We become people who live truthfully, not just because it's right, but because it honors the God we serve. We start walking in sexual purity, not just to avoid guilt, but because we recognize the sacredness of covenant and self-control. We forgive, even when it's hard, because the law has trained us to prioritize justice and mercy – not vengeance.

Obedience isn't a straitjacket. It's a compass.

It keeps us from getting lost in our own desires, our own excuses, our own self-justifying narratives. And let's be honest, we're all great storytellers when it comes to rationalizing sin. "I was tired." "They deserved it." "It's not that big of a deal."

But the law refuses to play along. It tells us the truth, even when we don't' want to hear it. It keeps calling us higher.

And that's exactly why we need it.

Because even in a world overflowing with opinions, what we're really lacking is conviction.

We need something stronger than the latest influencer's advice, or our own feelings on a Tuesday. We need a standard that doesn't shift based on circumstance, mood, or majority vote.

That's what the moral law provides. Not because it's legalistic, but because it's anchored.

And when we're anchored in God's truth, we're free to stop managing impressions and start pursuing holiness.

Let me pause here and say – this pursuit of holiness? It's not just for pastors, missionaries, or nuns. It's for accountants and teachers and stay-at-home moms. It's for high school students and Uber drivers and retired grandpas.

Holiness isn't about having a title or working in ministry. It's about responding to the God who rescued you with a life that says, "You're worthy of it all."

And the moral law is a beautiful starting point for that kind of response. It's where we learn what matters most in God's kingdom, truth, honor, worship, reverence, justice, purity, contentment, and love.

And here's the real kicker: the more we align with the moral law, the more free we actually become.

I know – sounds backwards. How can rules bring freedom?

But ask anyone who's lied their way into a corner, or lived with the guilt of betrayal, or chased covetousness until it swallowed their peace...They'll tell you: sin is a tyrant.

The enemy sells rebellion as freedom, but it always ends in chains.

Obedience, though? That's where true liberty lives.

Jesus said it this way:

"If ye continue in my word, then are ye my disciples indeed; And ye shall know the truth, and the truth shall make you free." John 8:31-32

Freedom doesn't come from doing whatever we want. It comes from being rightly ordered – spirit, soul, and body – under the rule of God.

The moral law helps us get there. It exposes the areas that still need reshaping. It guards us from self-destruction. It points us toward a better way.

And it's not a one-time lesson. We don't outgrow the Ten Commandments. We grow deeper into them.

Like a musician who keeps returning to scales, not because they're basic, but because they're foundational.

You never graduate from the basics of righteousness.

You just learn how to live them with more humility, more love, and more wisdom.

One day you realize you're not just avoiding sin, you're learning to love what's holy.

You're not just resisting lies; you're speaking truth with grace.

You're not just following rules, you're reflecting the Rulemaker.

That's the goal. Not moral superiority. Not self-congratulations. But transformation.

Not "Look how good I've been," but "Look how good God is to shape me like this."

And the more you walk that path, the more natural it becomes. Not effortless, but no longer foreign. Like learning a second language that eventually becomes your heart language.

The moral law may have started as a list, but in the life of a believer, it becomes something more – a lens. A rhythm. A way of seeing and living that brings clarity and confidence in a world full of noise.

One of the best things Jesus ever said about the law is also one of the most misunderstood.

"Think not that I am come to destroy the law, or the prophets: I am not come to destroy, but to fulfill." Matthew 5:17

In other words, He wasn't starting from scratch. He was picking up the whole story, fulfilling what was prophesied, and raising the bar, not lowering it. Jesus didn't loosen the moral law to make it easier for us to follow; He brought it into full focus.

Take adultery. The original command says, "Don't commit it." Jesus said if you look at someone with lust in your heart, you've already crossed the line.

Take murder. The command says, "Don't kill." Jesus said anger and contempt can be just as spiritually corrosive.

If anything, Jesus made it harder, not because He's mean or impossible to please, but because He's always been after the heart not just behaviour.

You can follow rules and still have a rotten soul.

Jesus knew this, and He confronted it over and over, especially with the Pharisees. These were the religious elites who had Scripture memorized but lacked mercy, justice, and humility. They tithed their herbs and spices with precision, but neglected the weightier matters of the law. They looked clean on the outside but were spiritually moldy on the inside.

In Matthew 23, Jesus didn't hold back. He called them hypocrites, blind guides, whitewashed tombs. Not because they loved the law – but because they weaponized it. They used it to prop up their egos instead of humbling their hearts.

That's the danger with moral knowledge. The more you know, the more tempted you are to measure others instead of yourself.

But Jesus, shows us a better way. He fulfilled the law by living it perfectly, not just outwardly, but in spirit, motive, and love. And then, in a stunning act of mercy, He died for those who couldn't live up to it. Which is...everyone.

Including us.

So now, when we read the moral law, we do so with realities in mind:

We fall short.

Christ fulfilled it for us – and is now forming it in us.

That's why we don't just throw our hands up and say, "Well, Jesus paid it all, so the law doesn't matter anymore." That's like saying, "Since my debt was paid, I'll just keep spending recklessly."

No, the gospel is an invitation to freedom, not foolishness.

The moral law doesn't threaten grace; it teaches us how to live in response to it.

Paul put it this way:

"What then? Shall we sin, because we are not under the law, but under grace? God forbid." Romans 6:15

Grace isn't a hall pass for sin. It's the power to walk in righteousness without the crushing weight of earning God's favor.

But let's acknowledge something hard: holding to a biblical moral standard will cost you something today. Sometimes, it'll cost a lot.

You'll be misunderstood, called judgemental for simply believing what the Bible says, be excluded, mocked, or labelled, and if you're not careful, you'll start to feel the pull to soften the message just enough to keep the peace.

But here's where Scripture anchors us. The moral law doesn't shift with opinion polls. It doesn't care about trending hashtags or academic theories. It stands firm, because it reflects the unchanging nature of God Himself.

And in a culture constantly redefining morality, your clarity will be a lighthouse. Not to condemn, but to guide.

Because people are drowning in a sea of choices. They're burnt out on doing what "feels right." They're desperate for something solid, something that doesn't move when they do.

And when your life reflects the stability of God's truth, it becomes strangely attractive, even if they don't admit it out loud.

That's how moral clarity becomes a witness. Not when it's shouted. But when it's lived.

When you're faithful in little things, refuse to lie on the resume, delete the flirtatious text, honor your word, even if it costs you. When you're kind in disagreement and pure in thought and treat holiness not as a chore, but as an act of worship.

That's when people start to wonder what's different about you. Not because you're morally superior, but because you're morally anchored.

You're not swept up in every new trend, not constantly shifting your boundaries, don't apologize for being faithful, and you don't walk around with a moral superiority complex, either.

You're just grounded.

And the root of that stability is the moral law alive in you, not because you've mastered it, but because you've surrendered to the One who did.

Let's make this practical. If you want to grow in biblical morality, start simple. Pick one commandment and ask:

What does this reveal about God's heart?

How does this shape how I treat others?

Where am I tempted to ignore or rationalize it?

What would obedience in this area look like today?

You don't have to fix everything at once. Growth isn't a microwave; it's a slow cooker. But if you keep returning to God's Word with a humble heart and a willing spirit, you'll start to notice change.

Not manufactured behaviour, but genuine transformation.

And when people ask what's changed, you won't have to deliver a theological lecture. You'll simply say, "God's been working on me. I'm learning to love what He loves."

That's what the moral law is about. Not control. Not comparison. Not spiritual report cards.

It's about love. Holiness. Honor. Wholeness.

And it still matters.

Even now. Especially now.

Let's be real: some people hear the word obedience and immediately think of childhood chores, military drills, or that one youth group leader who made everyone feel guilty for watching PG-13 movies. The idea of joyfully obeying God's moral law? It sounds...unlikely.

But that's because we've misunderstood obedience. We've treated it like a burden to bear instead of a blessing to walk in.

Obedience is not a punishment. It's a path. And the more we walk it, the more we realize it leads to freedom, not restriction.

Psalm 119, for example, is the longest chapter in the Bible. Do you know what it's about? The beauty of God's law. And it's not written by a spiritually dry person trudging through divine duty. It's a love song.

"O how love I thy law! It is my meditation all the day." Psalm 119:97

Not "Ugh, Your law is exhausting." Not "Fine, I'll obey so I don't get smited." Love. Delight. Joy.

Why? Because when God gives His commands, He's not trying to stifle our fun, He's protecting our flourishing.

God's laws don't just keep us from sin. They keep us from the pain, regret, shame, and self-inflicting chaos that sin brings with it.

If you've ever walked through the fallout of a lie, betrayal, addiction, or pride-fueled decision, you know this to be true. God's "thou shalt not" is often just another way of saying, "Please don't hurt yourself."

It's the loving voice of a Father saying, "Trust Me, this road leads to life. That one doesn't."

But still, there's this lingering temptation to treat obedience as a scoreboard. A way to earn favor. Prove yourself. Out-moral the next guy.

That's where legalism sneaks in – obedience divorced from relationship.

Legalism is like trying to win a spouse's love by following all the house rules. You might get points for loading the dishwasher, but if there's no actual intimacy, the relationship is cold.

God doesn't want your moral performance; He wants your heart.

Obedience, in its healthiest form, is a love response. Not a ladder to climb, but a posture of surrender.

You're not obeying because you're trying to be righteous. You're obeying because you already belong to the Righteous One. You've been loved, saved, forgiven, and now you're learning to walk like someone who's been made new.

And yes, some days you'll fall short. The old sin patterns will whisper. The flesh will pitch a fit. The temptation to cut corners will pop up like spiritual spam email.

But here's the beauty: repentance is always open.

That's another thing the moral law does; it reminds us how much we still need grace. Not just once, but every day. And grace is never in short supply.

Think of it like walking a trail with God. The moral law is the map. Grace is the guide. When you take a wrong turn, He doesn't leave you in the woods with a passive-aggressive sigh. He walks you back, restores your footing and says, "Let's keep going."

That's what keeps this from becoming exhausting.

Because without grace, the law becomes something far more beautiful, it becomes formational.

It shapes the kind of person you're becoming. Not just what you do, but how you think, how you react, how you handle tension.

For example, someone bumps into your life with offense or criticism. Without the moral law, your gut might say, "Snap back. Prove them wrong. Get the last word." But the law has trained your conscience: "Speak the truth but do it in love. Don't bear false witness. Don't let anger lead."

You begin to respond from conviction, not just emotion.

That's the fruit of obedience. It's not just about following commands; it's about becoming wise.

The world doesn't need more opinionated Christians. It needs wise ones. People who know the Word well enough to live it when things get messy.

Because let's face it – real-life morality doesn't usually show up in ten-second tests, it shows up in those long, drawn-out moments, where you're tired, stressed, misunderstood, or tempted.

When the deadlines closing in and cutting corners would make it easier, everyone's gossiping and you want to feel included, bitterness feels safer than forgiveness, and when scrolling into lust seems easier than self-control.

This is where the moral law, written on your heart, becomes more than just a principle. It becomes your compass.

Not just for avoiding sin, but for choosing holiness even when no one sees. And that? That's spiritual maturity. Not the flashy kind. The quiet kind. The kind that builds legacy, character, and trust over time.

One of the biggest lies we believe is that ethics are only for the big moments, "don't cheat on your spouse," "don't rob a bank," "don't become a dictator." But most of our moral life is built on small, daily choices that no one else sees.

And the moral law helps us treat those moments as sacred.

It whispers: "How you speak to your spouse matters. How you show up at work matters. What you do with your phone, your thoughts, your words, it all matters.

Why? Because it's forming the kind of person you're becoming when the big moments do come.

If you ignore the moral law in the small, you'll likely fail in the significant.

But when you practice righteousness in the everyday, you become strong for the trials you never saw coming.

That's the beauty of this entire system. God's moral law isn't just about what's right and wrong, it's about becoming someone who reflects Him. Not just once in a while, but consistently.

Obedience becomes a habit. Holiness becomes instinct. And grace fills the gap every time you stumble.

That's not religious performance. That's spiritual formation. And it's a life worth pursuing.

Sometimes when people talk about holiness, they get this serious tight-lipped look like they just bit into a lemon and forgot how joy works. Like God's goal is to make you boring, exhausted, and mildly judgemental. You know, "righteous."

But that's not the vibe we're going for.

Because real holiness, the kind rooted in God's moral law, isn't stale or stuffy. It's alive. It's joy-giving. And believe it or not, it actually makes life better.

Now I know what you're thinking. Better? Like kale better? Or actually better?

Stay with me.

Living according to the moral law doesn't mean you wake up every morning and think, "Ah yes, another chance to deny myself everything fun and holy, smile my way through traffic." No. It means you live with fewer regrets. Less relational drama. More peace. More sleep. (Because you're not lying awake wondering if someone's going to find out what you did.)

It means you walk around with integrity in your pocket, not shame.

And listen, you don't have to be morally perfect to enjoy this life. Just planted. You're learning. You're growing. You're putting your roots into something solid, so you're not blown over every time temptation rolls in with a cute smile or a "limited time only" discount.

That's what the moral law gives you, a strong spine in a world of spiritual jellyfish.

But let's not pretend it's easy. It's not like you wake up craving self-control or generosity.

Most of us don't naturally drift toward righteousness. We drift toward snacks, comfort, and soft pants.

You have to choose obedience. And half the time, you'll feel like the only one doing it.

You'll say no to something and immediately feel weird, because everyone else is saying yes. They're like, "It's not a big deal," and you're over here trying to remember what Leviticus said about motives and goat hair.

But this is where we stop and remind ourselves: the moral law was never meant to make us weird for weirds sake. It was meant to make us set apart. Different in a way that actually draws people in – not repels them with moral smugness and an unsolicited list of what we're against.

You know what's compelling?

When you're kind in tense situations. When you own your mistakes without blaming someone else. When you quietly choose what's right – even if no one claps. Especially when no one claps.

That's when the beauty of God's law shows up, not just in avoiding sin, but in living beautifully.

And let's not forget the gift of having clear moral lines in a world where most people are squinting through fog. You don't have to guess.

You don't have to crowdsource your ethics from strangers on the internet.

You've got a guidebook. And it's not outdated – it's timeless.

Take coveting, for example. That commandment feels like the quiet kid in the corner of the list, right? "Don't covet" seems so tame. But modern life is basically a coveting obstacle course.

Scroll through your feed: covet. Watch that home makeover show: covet. Hang out with a friend who just got a promotion and new teeth: covet.

God didn't forbid coveting because He's trying to ruin your dream board. He just knows comparison will rob your joy from the inside out.

And that's what so much of the moral law is, it's divine protection for your soul. It's not a checklist to earn gold stars; it's a set of guardrails so you don't drive your life off a cliff while trying to win at everything.

So, what does this actually look like?

It means you pause before responding. You ask yourself: Is this honest? Is this kind? Does this reflect Jesus or just my ego?

It means when you mess up (and you will), you don't pretend you didn't. You repent. Quickly. Honestly. And then you keep going.

It means you get used to choosing the narrow path, not because you love missing out, but because you've seen what's at the end of the wide one. Spoiler: it's not peace.

And most of all, it means you stop trying to be the moral police and start being a moral witness. Let your life speak. Let your choices preach. People don't need lectures, they need light.

So yes, God's moral law still matters. Yes, it's relevant. No, it's not too much. And yes, you can live it out in jeans, with coffee, in your real life.

Because holiness isn't about pretending to be perfect. It's about belonging to the One who is.

And from that place of belonging, you start to change. You start to want what He wants. You start to see obedience not as a cage, but as freedom. The kind that doesn't depend on how you feel that day. The kind that holds steady even when the world starts spinning.

Because let's be real: the world's spinning.

And what the world needs isn't more people who can quote Scripture with angry faces.

It needs people whose lives are so rooted in the goodness of God's law, so steady in truth and grace, that when others come unraveling, they know where to look.

Alright, friend – at this point, we've talked about a lot. The Ten Commandments, the heart behind the law, how Jesus fulfills it, how we're not supposed to treat holiness like a competition sport. It's been a journey. But before we land the plane, we've got to talk about something big.

What do we actually do with all this?

Because knowing that God's law is good and true is one thing. Letting it transform your everyday life? That's the actual work. And not the kind of work where you white-knuckle your way through every temptation with clenched teeth and a guilty conscience. I mean real transformation. Inside-out kind.

But here's where things get tricky. A lot of us, especially if we've been in church for more than five minutes, know how to talk about holiness. We know how to nod at the right moments, quote the right verses, and agree with the sermon points. We've got the language. But the law of God isn't just a topic to study, it's a lens we're meant to live through.

The truth, the more deeply God's moral law is written on your heart, the more it shows up where it really counts. In your habits, values, and your decisions when no one's watching.

And yes, even in those awkward conversations where you're the only person not cosigning the cultural narrative.

Let's say your coworkers are all on board with "everybody does it" ethics, the quiet lies on time sheets, the flirty messages on the side, the "I'm spiritual but not religious" brunch chats. If you're living out the moral law, you're going to stand out. Not because you're better, but because you're anchored.

You'll have moments when you don't get the invite because you're not the type to go with the flow. You'll find yourself biting your tongue, not out of fear, but out of wisdom. You'll feel a tug in your chest when the Spirit's like, "Hey, let's not do this the easy way. Let's do it the right way."

And some days, that'll feel like a buzzkill. But other days? It'll feel like freedom.

Because you're not chained to peer pressure anymore. You're not a slave to image maintenance or cultural applause. You've got something better: conviction and clarity.

Let me say this clearly because it's easy to forget, especially when your news feed is on fire and your inbox is full of passive-aggressive opinions:

You are allowed to walk in moral clarity without shame.

You don't have to apologize for believing what God said. You don't have to water it down, so people aren't uncomfortable.

You don't have to twist yourself into a theological pretzel trying to justify what Scripture clearly calls sin.

You can just...stand.

Not with arrogance. Not with smugness. Just steady. Planted. Rooted.

And when people ask why you don't play games, cheat, gossip, or fudge the truth like everyone else. That's your open door. You don't' need a full sermon. You just say, "Honestly, I'm trying to live according to God's Word. It matters to me."

Boom. That's it. No megaphone required.

Because here's the thing about moral consistency: it's rare. And people notice.

They may roll their eyes at first. But when life gets messy, and it always does, they'll remember you. The one who didn't flinch. The one who had boundaries, peace, and something solid beneath your feet.

This is how the law becomes more than theology. It becomes a testimony.

It becomes light.

And if you ever start to doubt whether it's worth it, just take inventory. Look at the people around you who don't have moral boundaries. Are they really thriving? Is all that self-made truth working out?

Usually not. Because when you make yourself your own authority, it's only a matter of time before you run out of wisdom.

That's why God's law is mercy in disguise.

It tells us, "You don't have to figure this out alone."

God isn't up in heaven waiting for you to mess it up so He can shame you. He's given you a framework, so you don't have to build your life on emotional guesswork and Instagram reels. You have something better.

You have truth. Anchored in love. Forged in holiness. Proven over centuries. And even when you mess up – which you will – He's not done with you.

Because grace walks hand in hand with truth. The law shows us the standard. Grace gives us the power to keep walking after we trip over it.

So no, you don't have to carry guilt like a backpack. And no, you don't have to pretend you've got it all together. But you can live with conviction.

And when you do?

Your life starts to sing a different tune.

People begin to feel it when they're around you. Not perfection – but presence. Not performance – but peace. Not fear – but faithfulness.

And they won't always know what to call it. But they'll want it.

So here we are, you and me, after thousands of words about ancient commands, modern lives, and how to love God without becoming a walking rulebook. We've walked through dusty scrolls and high-stakes moments, tiptoed around Pharisaical pitfalls, and hopefully laughed a little at ourselves along the way.

But now let's wrap it up.

Because the moral law, these commandments etched into stone thousands of years ago, are not just some OT relics to hang in courtrooms or teach in Workplace Safety Classes with a felt board Moses. They're a compass. A reflection. A mirror of the very character of God.

There is how He showed His people, "This is what I'm like. And this is how you can walk with Me."

And honestly, if we looked at them that way more often, we'd stop seeing them as a checklist and start seeing them as an invitation.

Because that's what they really are. An invitation to flourish. God's law says, "Here's the path. Walk in it. And when you trip, I'll help you up." Now sure, the law doesn't save you – only Jesus does that. But once you're His?

The law becomes like a guardrail on a cliff. Not to imprison you, but to protect you from the long, expensive fall of doing life your own way.

And don't miss this: the moral law isn't just about what you avoid. It's about who you're becoming.

A person who loves what God loves, who doesn't fold in the face of pressure, who stays rooted when the winds of culture blow wild, who can be trusted when no one's watching.

That's who God's forming you into. Not through a list of cold commands, but through a relationship that transforms how you live, how you think, and how you love.

And if we're being really honest, this kind of living stands out now more than ever. Because moral clarity isn't trending. Conviction isn't cool. And obeying ancient words from a holy God? Well, that'll get you labeled everything from old-fashioned to dangerous, depending on the day.

But that's okay. You weren't called to blend in. You were called to shine. And shining doesn't mean yelling. It doesn't mean policing everyone else's behaviour while ignoring your own. It means living in such a way that even people who disagree with you, respect the consistency in your life.

It means when the world says, "Just follow your heart," you say, "Actually, I'm going to follow God's heart instead. It's a little more reliable."

It means when others bend for convenience, you stay rooted in conviction. Not because you're better. But because you know where your help comes from.

Now if you're sitting here thinking, "Okay, this is inspiring, but what does obedience look like on a Tuesday?" – I'm so glad you asked.

It looks like faithfulness in the small things. The decisions that nobody tweets about. It's choosing to honor your spouse when they've annoyed you for the third time in an hour. It's paying the correct amount of taxes even when TurboTax finds a loophole. It's walking away from gossip at the table instead of contributing your spicy two cents.

It's not just what you do, it's how you do it. With grace. With humility. With a quiet strength that doesn't need a platform to prove it's real.

And here's what I love: the more you walk in obedience, the more natural it starts to feel. At first, it'll feel awkward – like wearing new shoes that haven't molded to your feet. But over time, it becomes second nature. Not because you're trying harder. But because your heart is changing.

Your spiritual taste bud's shift. You start craving truth more than validation. You start longing for peace more than popularity. You start loving holiness more than hype.

And before you know it, you're not just obeying the law. You're living in the freedom it was meant to bring. So don't shrink back from the moral law like it's some outdated burden you're stuck dragging through modern life. Stand tall in it. Delight in it. Let it remind you who God is – and who He's making you into. You're not perfect. You never will be. But you're not who you used to be, either.

You're someone being transformed, day by day, into a reflection of your holy Father. And that's no small thing.

The moral law isn't a relic. It's a rhythm. It's a revelation. It's part of the beautiful, holy story of how God makes people new.

And if you're walking with Him – guess what? You're part of that story, too.

So, stay rooted. Stay humble. Stay faithful. Because in a world of compromise, courage often looks like obedience.

And obedience? That still matters to God.

Even now.

Especially now.

Chapter 4:

The Teaching of Jesus and the Sermon on the Mount

You've got to hand it to Jesus, when He preached, He didn't exactly open with a crowd-pleaser. He didn't start the Sermon on the Mount with a list of miracles or a motivational quote. No drum roll, no Instagrammable one-liner. Just this:

"Blessed are the poor in spirit."

"Blessed are they that mourn."

"Blessed are the meek..."

If you're like most people, your first thought might be: "Blessed? That sounds like a therapy session, not a success strategy."

But that's the whole point.

The Beatitudes (Matthew 5:3-12) are Jesus' introduction to Kingdom living. And they sound nothing like what we're used to. They don't reward achievement, power, or confidence. They praise humility, brokenness, and mercy. They flip the moral scoreboard and hand gold medals to people the world barely notices.

It's like Jesus gathers His disciples, motions to the crowd, and says, "Okay – if you want to live by God's definition of good...it starts here. With the people no one celebrates."

Let's break it down. Because these statements aren't just poetic – they're ethical.

They tell us who we're called to be and what kind of heart God blesses.

"Blessed are the poor in spirit..."

Translation: the spiritually bankrupt. The ones who know they bring nothing to the table except need.

In a world obsessed with confidence and self-assurance, Jesus says, "Nope. I'm looking for humility." Not because God's into low self-esteem, but because He can work with people who know they're not the Savior of their own story.

This is the foundation of Kingdom Ethics: You're not the hero. You're the rescued.

"Blessed are the meek..."

Ah meekness – the fruit no one's adding to their dating profile. But in Kingdom math, meekness isn't weakness. It's power under control.

It's the ability to respond with gentleness when you could retaliate. To stay quiet when you could blast someone online. To absorb offense without letting it rot your soul.

Ethical living without meekness? That's just pride with a good memory.

"Blessed are they which do hunger and thirst after righteousness..."

Now this one slaps. Because Jesus doesn't say, "Blessed are the righteous." He says blessed are the ones who want it. Who crave right standing with God. Who can't settle for spiritual junk food anymore.

It's not about already having it all together – it's about being hungry for more of God, more holiness, more integrity.

You want to live rightly not because it's trendy (spoiler: it's not), but because you're spiritually starving without it.

"Blessed are the merciful..."

Okay, now it's getting real. Because being merciful isn't hard in theory, it's hard in traffic. It's hard when people fail you, hurt you, ghost you.

But mercy is how we reflect the heart of God. It's the refusal to reduce people to their worst moments. It's not turning a blind eye to sin but choosing not to weaponize justice like a bat.

Mercy says, "I've been shown grace, so I'm going to live like it."

"Blessed are the pure in heart…"

In other words, the ones who don't just look clean, they actually want to be clean. Jesus isn't impressed by whitewashed behaviour. He wants the real thing.

Purity of heart means your motives aren't always tangled up in people-pleasing, ego, or silent revenge plots.

You want to do what's right. Because it's right. Because it pleases God. Because you love Him, not because you want likes.

"Blessed are the peacemakers…"

Important note here: peacemaker is not the same as peacekeeper. One avoids conflict at all costs. The other engages with courage and grace to bring true reconciliation.

Peacemaking is risky. It means stepping into tension and working toward healing instead of pretending nothing's wrong.

And in a polarized world? That kind of courage is revolutionary.

"Blessed are they which are persecuted for righteousness' sake..."

And this is where Jesus really drops the mic. He's like, "Hey, by the way...if you do all this, you're going to get pushback."

If you live with moral clarity, don't be surprised if the world calls you names, mocks your convictions, or thinks you're just a killjoy with a Bible.

But Jesus doesn't say, "Tolerated are the persecuted." He says, "Blessed."

Why? Because it means you're doing something right.

Because standing for truth when it costs you something is one of the clearest signs that you belong to the Kingdom.

The Beatitudes aren't just a spiritual checklist; they're a portrait of the kind of people Jesus blessed.

And they turn our idea of "ethical success" upside down. In the Kingdom of God, greatness isn't defined by applause, it's defined by humility, mercy, purity, and courage.

Which means you don't have to be loud to be holy. You don't' need a platform to make a difference. You just need a heart that wants God more than approval.

That's where Christian ethics being – not with behaviour modification, but with heart transformation. And Jesus, being the brilliant Teacher that He is, starts there on purpose. He's not just giving us rules to follow. He's showing us a person to become.

One who looks suspiciously like Him.

So, imagine this; you're sitting on a hillside with Jesus, still trying to figure out what "poor in spirit" means, when He looks you straight in the eye and says:

"Ye are salt of the earth..."

"Ye are the light of the world..."

Matthew 5:13-14

Now, depending on your mood, that's either deeply encouraging or slightly terrifying. Salt of the whole earth? Light of the world? You might be thinking, "Jesus, I just figured out how to pray without getting distracted by birds. Maybe start off with 'light of the small village."

But that's the beauty of how Jesus teaches.

He doesn't just bless the meek, He gives them mission.

Let's start with salt. Back in Jesus' day, salt wasn't just something you sprinkled on fries. (Fries were not invented yet. Tragic times.)

Salt preserved food. It stopped meat from going rotten. It had value. It was even used as currency in some cultures.

So, when Jesus says you're the salt, He's saying:

"You stop the moral decay. You bring flavour to a bland, truth-starved world. You matter."

Now, here's where it gets personal. Because if you're salt, then your life is supposed to make things better around you. Not by being the loudest person in the room, but by being anchored in truth. By refusing to rot with the rest of the meat, if you will.

Salt doesn't make a scene. It works quietly, but powerfully.

You know when it's missing. You also know when there's too much of it. (See also: that one overzealous Bible guy at every holiday gathering.)

Jesus gives a warning too:

"But if the salt have lost his savour, wherewith shall it be salted?"

Oof. In other words, what good is salt that doesn't taste like salt? What's the point of a believer who doesn't live any differently than the world around them?

When your morals are no longer distinct, when you blur the lines, dull the flavour, bend in, to avoid pushback, you lose the very thing that made you vulnerable in the first place.

This isn't about perfection. It's about preservation.

Your character is part of God's mercy to the world. You may not see it, but every time you stand for integrity, show grace, resist gossip, or choose the high road – you're keeping spiritual decay at bay. You're slowing the rot.

And honestly? That matters.

Then Jesus hits us with Light.

"Ye are the light of the world A city that is set on an hill cannot be hid."

Again, no pressure, right? Just the light of the whole world.

But let's unpack this because it's more comforting than intimidating.

When Jesus calls you "light," He's not expecting you to manufacture your own glow. He's not saying, "Try really hard to be radiant." He's saying, "Stay close to Me – the Light – and reflect what I give you."

Light doesn't argue with darkness. It just shows up.

And when it does, things are seen clearly. Corners get exposed. Clarity begins. Sometimes that makes people uncomfortable. (Let's be honest, most of us prefer dim lighting when we're not proud of what's going on.)

But light doesn't come to shame. It comes to reveal, to heal, to guide.

Your life, lived in truth, humility, and love – is meant to be a lighthouse. Not a searchlight, scanning for everyone else's sin. Just steady, visible faithfulness

That alone will draw people to Jesus more than a hundred clever Instagram reels ever could.

Jesus goes on:

"Neither do men light a candle, and put it under a bushel, but on a candlestick..."

Translation: don't hide your light.

Don't dim your faith to fit in. Don't water down the truth to keep peace. Don't bury your convictions in a drawer labeled "Too Awkward to Share."

If you believe that the gospel changes everything (and it does), then people should see that difference in you. Not because you're trying to perform, but because it's become who you are.

And here's the kicker:

"Let your light so shine before men, that they may see your good works, and glorify your Father…"

That's the goal. No spotlighting you. Glorifying Him.

Not "look how good I am," but "look how good God is to make someone like me walk in truth and love."

That's how Christian ethics becomes a witness, not just a lifestyle, but a testimony.

You're not salt and light because you have all the answers. You're salt and light because Jesus is in you, and you're learning to live like that actually means something.

So, friend, let's pull it all together.

Salt doesn't rot. Light doesn't hide. And you, flawed and growing as you are, have been chosen to show the world what Jesus is like.

Not by arguing louder, or by posting more Scripture in all-caps, but by living a life so full of integrity, grace, humility, and consistency…people can't help but see something holy in it.

That's what Christian ethics looks like with a flashlight in one hand and seasoning in the other.

It's practical. It's powerful. And it's your calling.

Let it shine.

Okay, confession time. If Jesus had just said, "Be nice to people and don't murder anyone," we'd be golden. Most of us aren't out here plotting homicides. But that's not what He said.

Instead, He looked at a crowd of people, including folks who were probably pretty proud of their moral record, and said something like:

"You've heard it said...don't kill anybody. But I say...don't even stay angry."

"You've heard it said...don't commit adultery. But I say...don't even look with lust."

Insert nervous chuckle here.

Suddenly it's not about just what you do. It's about what's going on inside your chest.

Jesus wasn't raising the standards to be dramatic. He was revealing what had always been true: God isn't after behaviour modification. He's after heart transformation.

Which is both beautiful and terrifying, depending on what's currently living rent-free in your heart.

Here's how it worked back then: the Pharisees were the moral elite. These guys nailed the external stuff. They tithed down to the spice rack.

They fasted, prayed, kept every visible part of the law. But Jesus said their righteousness wasn't enough.

"Except your righteousness shall exceed the righteousness of the scribes and Pharisees, ye shall in no case enter into the kingdom of heaven." Matthew 5:20

Now hold on. That would've stunned the audience. How do you top the spiritual honor roles?

Simple. You stop trying to impress people and start living honestly before God.

Jesus was calling out the great ethical illusion: that you can look holy without being holy. That you can technically follow the rules while your heart is a toxic dumpster fire of pride, envy, and contempt.

But let's be honest – we've all been there.

We haven't killed anyone, but we've assassinated someone's character in a group chat.

We haven't cheated on our spouse, but we've daydreamed our way through entire movie plots, starring that one person we know we shouldn't be thinking about.

We haven't broken into a store, but we've justified keeping money that wasn't really ours, or shading the truth on a form "just a little."

And Jesus goes, "Yeah, let's talk about that."

Not to shame us, but to free us.

Because you can never grow out of what you won't admit.

Here's the thing, Jesus isn't being nitpicky. He's being loving. He's exposing the root, so you don't keep dealing with the same rotten fruit.

If He only cared about external obedience, He'd have passed out gold stars for showing up to synagogue on time and never using your oxen on the Sabbath.

But instead, He says, "Let's go deeper."

"You angry? Let's deal with that before it turns into bitterness."

"Looking a little too long? Let's redirect your eyes before your heart follows."

"Making oaths to sound spiritual? Let your 'yes' be 'yes,' and your 'no,' be 'no.' Stop performing."

Because the performance might fool people. But it doesn't form you.

So, what's the practical takeaway?

Jesus calls you to a higher standard, yes – but He also gives you a new heart to live it out.

You're not left white-knuckling your way through every lustful thought or biting your tongue until it bleeds. You're invited to bring your whole messy, needy self to Him, daily, and ask for help for strength. For conviction. For grace.

You know what's refreshing? Jesus is the only one who can call you higher without crushing you in the process.

He doesn't dangle the standard over your head like, "Good luck, sinner!" He says, "I'm with you. I fulfilled the law, and now I'm going to write it on your heart."

That means you're not obeying to earn His love. You're obeying because you already have it, and now you want to walk in a way that reflects who He is.

Now, let's not sugarcoat this.

Living at the heart level is harder. It's messier. It requires self-awareness and humility and a willingness to change when the Holy Spirit gently points out something gross in you.

But the reward? It's integrity. Real character. Not just a reputation for being "a good person," but the actual fruit of a life lived close to Jesus.

And that kind of righteousness? That's rare. But it's world-changing.

It's the kind that makes people wonder how you stay so grounded in chaos. It's the kind that keeps your marriage strong when others are falling apart.

It's the kind that helps you own your mistakes, forgive deeply, serve joyfully, and speak the truth when it's easier to stay silent.

This is what happens when ethics moves from paper to personhood. You become someone who doesn't just believe in the moral law. You embody it. Quietly. Consistently. And with grace for yourself when you stumble.

Because the Christian life isn't about being spotless, it's about being surrendered.

So, yes – Jesus raised the bar.

But not to make you feel like a failure.

He raised it to show you what real holiness looks like, and then gave you the Spirit so you could actually walk it out...

One choice. One thought. One surrendered heart at a time.

Here's the thing about Jesus: He wasn't impressed with religious theater.

You could fast until your stomach growled in Hebrew, pray loud enough to echo down the street, or give so much away your wallet developed separation anxiety...and He still wasn't clapping.

Why? Because in the Kingdom of God, motive matters.

Let's go to Matthew 6, where Jesus takes a loving sledgehammer to every self-righteous performance strategy:

"Take heed that ye do not your alms before men, to be seen of them..."
"When thou doest alms, let not thy left hand know what thy right hand doeth..."
"When thou prayest, enter into the closet..."
"When ye fast, be not...of a sad countenance..."
Matthew 6:1-18

Now before we start handing out awards for who can pray the quietest or sneak their giving in the most discreet envelope, let's pause.

Jesus isn't saying public acts of faith are bad.

He's saying performing righteousness for applause is empty.

It's spiritually cosplay.

It might get you followers. It might impress your small group. It might even go viral on Christian TikTok. But in heaven's accounting system?

Jesus says, "You've already got your reward." And spoiler alert – it's small, cheap, and temporary.

Let's break it down real quick:

Giving.

Jesus says don't give like you're narrating your own generosity, "Behold, as I donate this humble sum to the needy, please enjoy this slow-motion video with dramatic music…"

Just give. Quietly. Faithfully. With joy. Because God sees what you do in secret, and He's not grading on production value.

Prayer.

Again, nothing wrong with public prayer. But if your prayer voice changes into OT prophet mode the moment people are listening, maybe…take it down a notch.

Jesus isn't impressed by fancy phrases. He says go into your room, shut the door, and talk to your Father. Not your audience. Not your followers. Just Him.

Simple. Honest. Sincere.

Fasting.

This one gets overlooked, but Jesus goes there. Don't fast with a spiritual pout. Don't walk into work like, "I'm fine. Just deeply suffering for Jesus. No big deal."

Wash your face. Get dressed. And don't make your hunger your headline.

Why? Because the goal of fasting isn't sympathy, it's intimacy. You're not trying to earn points. You're making space for God.

So, here's the big takeaway.

God isn't looking for spiritual performers. He's looking for surrendered people.

You can do the right thing for the wrong reason and miss the heart of God entirely. Thinks about it: if you gave your spouse flowers every week, but only because you wanted to post about it online, how romantic would that feel?

Exactly.

But if you brought home a bouquet just because you love them, no posts, no crowd, just presence, that's different. That's intimate. That's relationship.

That's what God wants with you.

And this really matters when we talk about Christian ethics.

Because some people treat ethics like a brand. A curated lifestyle. A checklist they flash when applying for church leadership or dating someone with high standards.

But if it's not coming from your heart, if it's not rooted in actual relationship with God – it's not righteousness. It's religion with stage lights.

You know the difference, too.

One is exhausting. You're constantly monitoring how holy you look instead of who you're becoming.

The other is freeing. You're not trying to prove anything – you're just walking with your Father.

And when you get that?

You stop needing to appear righteous...because you're learning to be actually righteous.

Even when no one sees, when it costs you something, when your name never gets mentioned.

Because you're not working for applause. You're living for His smile.

Here's what this looks like in real life.

You delete the sarcastic comment you were proud of before you post it. You show up early to serve, and no one but Jesus knows. You resist the urge to name-drop your giving, your fast, your sacrifice. You're kind to the person no one else notices, not for points, just for love.

And slowly, your heart softens. Your motives align. You begin to enjoy righteousness for its own sake, not as a flex, but as a fruit.

It's quiet. It's deep. It's beautiful.

Let's be clear: you're never going to have perfect motives. This isn't about obsessing over every internal impulse.

But it is about being honest with God.

"Lord, I want to please You – not just perform. Help my heart match my actions."

That's the prayer He always honors.

Because when you live for God's glory instead of human applause, your life gets lighter. You don't need constant validation. You don't need the stage. You just need His presence.

And ironically? That's when you shine brightest.

Not because you're trying to, just because you're real.

Let's talk about your heart. Not the beating organ, but the part of you that obsesses over Amazon carts, job titles, followers, vacation photos, retirement plans, and what everyone else is doing better than you.

Yea. That heart.

Because Jesus gets it. He knows how easy it is to say you love God, while secretly trusting money to make you feel safe. Or chasing stuff to feel significant. Or scrolling endlessly to fill some vague sense of not-enough-ness you can't even name.

So, He drops this line, one of the simplest and most world-rocking things He ever said:

"For where your treasure is, there will your heart be also." Matthew 6:21

Boom. Conviction in one sentence.

Jesus doesn't say your heart should be where your treasure is. He says it already is. Your heart is following your treasure like a toddler with sticky fingers. Whatever you value most? That's where your soul is camping out.

So, the real ethical question isn't just, "What do I believe?" It's, "What do I love?"

Because your choices, your priorities, your calendar, your budget, your peace level, all tell a story about your treasure.

And here's what makes this tough: the things we treasure aren't always evil. A nice house? Cool.

A steady paycheck? Great. Security, stability, a decent Wi-Fi signal? All fine things.

But when they become the foundation of your identity, or the measuring stick for your worth? That's when you start to wobble.

That's why Jesus tells us: "Lay not up for yourselves treasures upon earth..."

Because earthly treasure? It rots. It gets stolen, hacked, canceled, unfollowed, or eaten by time and termites.

But treasure in heaven? Untouchable.

He's not saying sell everything and go live in the woods with a goat named Ezekiel. (Unless you're into that.) He's saying: store up stuff that lasts.

Things like faithfulness. Generosity. Kindness. Truth. Love. Obedience.

These are the treasures that don't show up on your tax return but ring loudly in eternity.

Now, Jesus doesn't stop there. He knows that behind our love of stuff is something deeper: worry.

Because when your treasures in the wrong place, your peace is fragile.

It can be stolen just as quickly as your identity when you click the wrong link.

So, Jesus says:

"Take no thought for your life, what ye shall eat, or what ye shall drink...Is not the life more than meat, and the body than raiment?" Matthew 6:25

In other words: chill. Your Father knows what you need.

Look at the birds, Jesus says. They don't have 401Ks. They're not hoarding seeds in climate-controlled bins. Yet God feeds them.

Look at the lilies. They're not frantically checking Pinterest for the latest outfit inspo. And yet Solomon, with all his royal stylists, never looked that fresh.

And here's the mic drop: "Are ye not much better than they?"

Of course you are.

God made you in His image. Called you by name. Send His Son for you. And He's going to forget about your grocery bill?

Not a chance.

But worry convinces us otherwise.

Worry is that little voice that says, "What if He doesn't show up this time? What if He forgets you?" And Jesus is like, "I feed birds. I clothe flowers. You think I'm going to ghost you?"

Please.

But here's the twist: worry and worship can't share the same space.

You're either trusting God, or you're trusting yourself. And spoiler: one of those is not qualified to carry the weight of your entire life.

Jesus gets super practical here:

"See ye first the kingdom of God, and his righteousness; and all these things shall be added unto you." Matthew 6:33

This is ethics in motion. Jesus says if you want your life to be right ordered – if you want your heart to be clear, your choices grounded, your priorities wise, seek God first.

Not your plan, success, or perfect morning routines with lemon water and five devotionals.

Seek Him.

And everything else? It falls into place.

Not magically. Not without effort. But without fear. And that's the difference.

Because kingdom priorities don't mean you stop working or planning or stewarding well. They just mean you no longer panic when things feel out of control.

You've got a new center. A new gravity. A new King. And with Him on the throne, you don't have to chase after things the way the world does.

You don't have to be owned by your ambition, have to spiral when the market drops, have to compare your story to the highlight reels around you.

You can breathe. You can trust. You can live light.

Because if your treasure is in the Kingdom, your heart will follow, and so will your peace.

If you've spent more than five minutes online, or say, disagreed with someone at a family dinner, you've probably heard it:

"You can't judge me! Jesus said so!"

And they're not totally wrong. Jesus did say that. It's just.... not the only thing He said.

Because context matters. And pulling, "judge not" out of Matthew 7 without reading the rest of the paragraph is kind of like quoting "thou shalt not kill" while setting up a paintball sniper in youth group.

Let's read it the way Jesus gave it:

"Judge not, that ye be not judged. For with what judgement ye judge, ye shall be judged: and with what measure ye mete, it shall be measured to you again. And why beholdest thou the mote that is in thy brother's eye, but considerest not the beam that is in thine own eye?" Matthew 7:1-3

Let's pause for a second.

Jesus is not saying, "Don't ever tell anyone they're wrong," He's saying, "Don't be a hypocrite about it."

The person He's calling out is the one who's all up in someone else's spiritual eyelash, while dragging a giant piece of lumber out of the side of their head. (Frankly, if you ever wanted biblical support for "mind your own business until you get your act together," here it is.)

This passage isn't about never correcting, it's about how and why we correct.

Here's the deal: Judgement without humility is toxic. Correction without love is a sledgehammer. And spiritual rebuke without self-awareness? That's just a fancy way of being a jerk for Jesus.

That's why Jesus follows up with this instruction:

"First cast out the beam out of thine own eye; and then shalt thou see clearly to cast out the mote out of thy brother's eye." Matthew 7:5

See it?

He's not saying ignore your brother's issues. He's saying start with your own. Clear your own vision before trying to fix someone else's.

That's not softness. That's wisdom.

You can't call someone toward holiness while tripping over your own unrepentance.

So, before you point fingers ask questions like:

Am I walking in humility right now?

Do I actually care about this person – or just about being right?

Have I invited the Holy Spirit to check me first?

If the answer to those is "yes," then – and only then – you're in a place to help a brother or sister see more clearly. Not to shame them. Not to win an argument. But to restore, gently, like Scripture teaches. (Galatians 6:1)

Let's talk tone for a minute.

Because in the church world, "truth-tellers" often pride themselves on being blunt. "I just say it like it is," they'll say. Or "God called me to be prophetic."

Cool. But Jesus called us to be Christlike. And that includes how we speak.

There's a big difference between correction and condemnation.

Correction says, "You're drifting – I want to help you come home."

Condemnation says, "You're messed up and I'm done with you."

Only one of those reflects the heart of Jesus.

He didn't come swinging a stick. He came with truth and grace, never one without the other. He ate with sinners, forgave those caught in the act, and saved His strongest rebukes for the religious folks who looked down on everyone else.

That should tell us something.

Now, one more verse gets squeezed into this passage that seems a little out of place at first:

"Give not that which is holy unto the dogs, neither cast ye your pearls before swine..."
Matthew 7:6

Wait – did Jesus just call people pigs and dogs? Kind of. But again, context.

He's saying there's a time to walk away.

Sometimes, your correction – however gentle and well-intentioned – isn't received because the person's heart isn't open. And when that's the case, you're not obligated to keep force-feeding truth to someone who's just going to trample it.

That's not judgement. That's discernment.

Jesus knew that not every seed would fall on good soil. He even warned His disciples that some people would reject them completely. That's not failure. That's reality.

So, part of living ethically is knowing when to speak, and when to be silent.

Alright, let's land this:

If you want to live the ethical life Jesus describes in the Sermon on the Mount, you have to be willing to see clearly. That means letting God deal with your heart first. Not in a self-shaming way, but in a humble, honest, "Lord, search me" way.

Then, when you do step into hard conversations or offer loving correction, it's not from a high horse – it's from level ground.

Because the goal isn't to win.

The goal is restoration.

The goal is clarity and healing and wholeness.

The goal is to be the kind of person who can say hard things softly – because you've wrestled with your own sin, and you've met grace there.

And when the Spirit leads you to speak?

Speak. Gently. Boldly. Lovingly.

Not to show how holy you are. But to show how faithful God is.

By this point in the Sermon on the Mount, Jesus has already flipped everyone's ethical expectations upside down.

And just when you think He might end with a nice motivational thought, He says something...a little unnerving.

"Enter ye in at the strait gate: for wide is the gate, and broad is the way, that leadeth to destruction...and many there be which go in thereat." Matthew 7:13

Yikes. Not exactly the "Live, Laugh, Love" aesthetic we were hoping for.

But this is classic Jesus – loving enough to be honest.

He's warning us: the way of the Kingdom isn't the way of the crowd.

The broad road? That's the path of moral convenience. It's the ethics of "just follow your heart," "be true to yourself," "you do you." No confrontation. No conviction. No cost.

But the narrow road? That's the path of obedience, integrity, and surrender.

And here's the kicker – it doesn't feel crowded. Sometimes you'll feel like the only one saying no when everyone's shouting yes. The only one holding to truth when it's not popular. The only one who seems to care about what God says.

That's okay. You're in good company.

The narrow gate was never about being exclusive for the sake of exclusion, it's just that few people are willing to take the road of real repentance and humble trust.

But Jesus is at the end of that road. And that's worth everything.

And then, just when you're bracing yourself for more narrow-gate content, Jesus drops this:

"Beware of false prophets, which come to you in sheep's clothing, but inwardly they are ravening wolves." Matthew 7:15

So now we've got narrow gates and wolves? Great.

But here's what He's saying: not everyone who uses God's name speaks with His voice.

That's heavy. And it means if we're going to live ethically, we have to be discerning.

Because wolves don't show up with pitchforks and name tags that say "Heretic." They come dressed as friends, leaders, influencers, authors, and even pastors – sometimes quoting Scripture while distorting the message.

So, how do you spot one?

"Ye shall know them by their fruit." Matthew 7:16

Jesus is giving us a Kingdom ethics field test. Don't just look at their charisma. Look at their character.

Are they humble or self-promoting?

Do they live what they preach?

Does their message draw people to Jesus – or just to themselves.

Because anyone can have a platform. But only the Spirit can produce real fruit.

And right in the middle of this warning, Jesus gives the ethical gold standard we all learned in kindergarten (but still struggle with as adults):

"Therefore all things whatsoever ye would that men should do to you, do ye even so to them..." Matthew 7:12

The Golden Rule. Simple. Brilliant. Underrated.

It's not "treat others how they deserve." It's "treat them how you want to be treated."

Not based on their behaviour, but on your values.

That means loving when it's not returned. Serving when it's not noticed. Forgiving when it's not asked for. Respecting when it's not earned.

Not because they deserve it. But because Jesus commands it and modeled it.

That's Kingdom ethics in a sentence. Live toward others the way you want God to live toward you.

And trust me, He's watching not just what you do, but why you do it.

Jesus finishes His sermon with one final image. And it's not theoretical. It's painfully practical.

He tells the story of two builders.

One built his house on rock. The other on sand. At first, both houses probably looked pretty good. Clean lines. Fresh paint. Instagram worthy décor.

But then the storm came.

And the house on sand? Total collapse. The house on the rocks? Still standing.

Here's how Jesus explains it:

"Whosoever heareth these sayings of mine, and doeth them, I will liken him unto a wise man..." Matthew 7:24

Notice the key: hearing and doing.

You can go to every Bible study, read every theology book, memorize the Sermon on the Mount – and still crumble – if you don't actually obey what Jesus said.

Christian ethics isn't just about knowing the truth. It's about living it. That's what makes your life storm-proof.

Not perfect circumstances. Not constant spiritual highs. But consistent, quiet obedience when it's hard. When it's costly. When no one's clapping.

That's what builds a foundation.

And storms will come.

The storm of temptation, rejection, disappointment, being misunderstood or misaligned for standing firm on biblical truth.

They're coming. Not "if" – but – "when."

And when they hit, you'll discover what kind of life you've built.

Was it polished but hollow? All talk, no trust? Or was it planted deep in the bedrock of God's Word?

This is why Jesus closes the greatest sermon ever preached not with poetry or a pep talk, but with a call to action.

Live this out.

Don't just admire it. Don't just quote it. Build your life on it. Because when winds show and the rain falls and the culture shifts and the pressure mounts, those who stand are not the smartest or the loudest.

They're the ones who obeyed.

So, here's the final word:

If you want to live a moral, ethical, Kingdom life in a noisy world, compromised, trend-obsessed world...

Listen closely. Love sincerely. Repent quickly. Forgive freely. Tell the truth. Stay humble. Love holy. Stay rooted.

Because those who build on the Rock?

They don't just survive the storm.

They stand strong in it.

Chapter 5:

The Role of the Holy Spirit in Christian Ethics

So, here's a confession: I used to think being a good Christian just meant trying harder.

And let's be honest for a second: being "good" is exhausting.

Trying to do the right thing all the time can feel like trying to juggle flaming swords while riding a unicycle in a thunderstorm. You smile at the annoying co-worker. You grit your teeth through traffic instead of saying what you really want to say. You try and forgive the person who borrowed your favorite book and never gave it back. And all the while, you're wondering, "Is this what God meant by holy?"

Somewhere along the way, many of us absorbed this idea that Christian ethics means constantly policing our thoughts, controlling our impulses, and stuffing our bad attitudes into a spiritual junk drawer until company leaves. But here's the catch, eventually that drawer pops open.

That's where the Holy Spirit steps in.

He's not the spiritual janitor cleaning up our messes. He's not the guilt tripper, the cosmic micromanager, or the background music to your Bible reading. He's God. Active, alive, personal, present. And He's not just walking alongside you; He's living in you. Not to haunt your conscience – but to shape your character.

Christian ethics isn't about perfect behaviour. It's about Spirit-formed living. And you can't pull that off with just elbow grease and coffee-fueled willpower.

Let's back up.

When Jesus walked the earth, He did something incredible – He taught people what God was like. Not just in ideas, but in action. He flipped over tables in the temple and fed hungry crowds. He told the truth with power, but never without compassion. He lived what we're trying to become: a life full of grace and truth.

Then, before He left, He told His disciples something that still feels wild if you think about it:

"It is expedient for you, that I go away...for if I go not away, the Comforter will not come unto you." John 16:7

Hold up. Better than Jesus with us is the Spirit in us?

Yes. That's what He said. Jesus went to the Father so the Spirit could come dwell within every believer, not just the lucky ones walking dusty roads in sandals 2,000 years ago. That means you and I, don't get the downgraded version of God. We get the full, personal presence of God – forever, wherever we go.

But who exactly is the Holy Spirit?

Let's clear up a few misconceptions.

The Holy Spirit is not a vibe. Not a mist. Not a spiritual energy that floats around and occasionally zaps people into doing something dramatic during worship. He is a person. The third person of the Trinity. Co-equal with the Father and the Son. He is the Spirit of truth, the Spirit of power, the Spirit of Christ. He is not weird. People can be weird. But the Holy Spirit is holy, and gloriously, beautifully normal in the life of a believer.

He convicts, yes. But He also comforts. He leads and teaches, intercedes, warns, reveals, and strengthens. The same Spirit that raised Jesus from the dead is now the One living inside of you. And not as a guest – He brought a change of address. You're His home now.

So why does it matter for Christian ethics?

Because trying to live ethically without the Holy Spirit is like trying to bake a cake without heat. You might have all the right ingredients, the rules, the knowledge, the intention, but without the transformative power of the Spirit, it's all just cold batter.

That's what Paul talks about in Romans. He doesn't say, "The key to godly living is trying really hard to follow the law."

In fact, he says the opposite. The law – while good – only showed us how messed up we really are. It pointed out the cancer. But it couldn't cure it.

What does cure it?

"The law of the Spirit of life in Christ Jesus hath made me free from the law of sin and death." Romans 8:2

This is the shift. From law to life. From external pressure to internal transformation.

The Holy Spirit doesn't just demand holiness, He produces it.

That means when you mess up, you don't run from God in shame. You run to Him, where the Spirit is already ready to walk you through repentance and restoration. Conviction isn't God's way of punishing you. It's His invitation to come home.

It's the nudge you feel when you're about to say something you'll regret. It's the discomfort you feel when you're trying to justify something shady. It's the still, small voice saying, "There's a better way." Not the guilt-trip you, but to guide you.

Conviction and condemnation are two different things. And knowing the difference is crucial.

Condemnation says, "You failed, you're trash, and God's probably tired of you."

Conviction says, "That wasn't right, and I love you too much to let you stay there."

One voice pushes you into hiding. The other invites you into healing.

The Holy Spirit is not your spiritual parole officer, waiting for you to slip up. He's your Advocate. Your Helper. Your Counselor. And He is radically committed to your transformation.

That transformation? It's not always instant. (If only.)

Sometimes it's so slow, it feels like you're just circling the same mountain over and over again. But if you pay attention, you'll notice that your reactions are changing. Your instincts are maturing. That thing that used to set you off doesn't anymore. That temptation that once had you in a chokehold now passes like a cloud. That's not random. That's fruit.

You've probably heard of the fruit of the Spirit, love, joy, peace, patience, kindness, goodness, faithfulness, gentleness, and self-control.

That list isn't a motivational poster. It's the natural outflow of a life that stays connected to the Vine. You don't grow fruit by straining. You grow it by abiding.

The Spirit cultivates these things over time, and they become your new ethical reflexes.

You used to snap back when someone disrespected you. Now, you breathe and respond in peace.

You used to shade the truth when it made you look better. Now, you speak honestly, even when it costs you. You used to avoid conversations. Now, you walk into them with love and clarity.

That's fruit. That's transformation. That's the Holy Spirit doing what no checklist ever could.

He's not making you a rule-follower. He's making you like Christ. And guess what? He's also making you wise.

The Holy Spirit doesn't just help you act right. He helps you discern right. Because let's be honest, life isn't always black and white. Sometimes you're faced with situations that Scripture doesn't explicitly cover. Do I take this job? Do I date this person? Do I call out this injustice or keep quiet? There's no verse that says, "Thou shalt take the marketing position in Austin."

That's where the Spirit leads. He whispers peace when you're in the will of God and stirs up unrest when something's off. He helps you interpret your motives, untangle your emotions, and choose integrity when it's easier to fake it.

But here's the thing: He doesn't shout over the noise. You've got to slow down enough to listen.

He speaks in the quiet. In the Word. In the space between distractions. And if you give Him attention, He'll give you, His direction.

This kind of Spirit-led living isn't reserved for the "super spiritual." It's for every believer. Every day. You don't need a prophetic anointing or a seminary degree. You need a surrendered heart and an open ear.

You may still make mistakes. You might miss a nudge here or there. But the Spirit is not looking for flawless execution. He's looking for faithful connection.

He doesn't ditch you when you stumble. He's there when you confess. When you cry. When you try again.

He's the One who reminds you of your identity when you forget. He's the One who gives you power when your flesh is screaming.

He's the One who helps you walk out your "yes" to Jesus when everything in you wants to quit.

That's not emotional hype. That's the real faithful work of the Spirit.

And it's the only way Christian ethics becomes more than a philosophy – it becomes a lifestyle.

A Spirit-led, peace-driven, fruit-producing, holiness-reflecting lifestyle that points people not to you, but to the One who's making all things new – including you.

So now we've established that the Holy Spirit empowers ethical living, grows fruit in us, and helps us discern in the gray areas, but there's more. Because the Spirit doesn't just guide your behaviour; He actually renovates your entire inner life.

And He starts with your mind.

Romans 12:2 says, "Be ye transformed by the renewing of your mind." That word "renewing" is the key here. You're not just cleaning house. You're getting a whole new blueprint. The Spirit doesn't slap duct tape on broken thought patterns. He rebuilds them from the ground up.

The world teaches you to be suspicious, the Spirit teaches you to believe the best.

The world says, "Look out for number one," the Spirit says, "Lay your life down."

The world applauds self-promotion, the Spirit teaches humility, and not the false kind that just wants to be praised for being humble. The real kind that forgets itself altogether.

And this renewed mindset spills out into your speech, your motives, your relationships, your integrity...even your calendar.

Suddenly, your decisions are less about what's convenient and more about what's obedient. Less about what impresses people and more about what pleases God.

That's the kind of inner shift no self-help book can pull off. Only the Spirit can do that. But He doesn't do it without your cooperation.

This is what the phrase "walking in the Spirit" comes into play. You've heard it. Maybe you've even said it. But what does it actually mean?

It doesn't mean floating through life in a spiritual trance, hearing the audible voice of God every five minutes. It means being responsive. Yielded. It means living aware that God is present, and active, in your every moment.

You walk in the Spirit by inviting Him into your actual life. Not just your Sunday morning "church face," but your Tuesday board meeting, your Thursday night family dinner, your Saturday Walmart run. You ask for His wisdom when you're frustrated. You listen when He brings someone to mind. You pause before responding with sarcasm (even when it's deserved.) You forgive, not because you feel like it, but because He reminds you how much you've been forgiven.

That's Spirit-led living. It's not flashy. It's faithful.

And honestly, it's counterculture.

Because let's face it, everything around you is screaming, "Follow your heart!" "Do what makes you happy!" "Speak your truth!"

But the Spirit says, "Follow Jesus," "Do what's holy." "Speak the truth, in love."

Those messages don't always land you in the spotlight. Sometimes they land you in isolation. The ethical path rarely wins popularity contests. But it will always win in the presence of God.

And here's something else the Spirit does, something subtle, but powerful. He helps you become a non-anxious-presence in an anxious world.

When the news cycle spins, when everyone's offended, when decisions feel weighty and the stakes are high, the Spirit steadies you. You don't have to panic, because you have a peace that's not based on circumstances. That peace isn't your own; it's His. A fruit of the Spirit. A shield for your mind. A signpost that you belong to a different Kingdom.

And you know what else?

The Spirit gives you courage.

Not the kind that roars from stages or posts viral monologues on social media. The kind that stays. The kind that chooses faithfulness when compromise would be easier.

The kind that speaks the truth in quiet rooms. The kind that says, "I'd rather lose status than lose integrity."

Because sometimes the most courageous thing you can do is just keep showing up, rooted, obedient, consistent, and kind.

That's not weakness. That's Spirit-filled grit.

It's what helps you stay ethical in the places no one else sees – when you're alone in your car, reading that email, you're deciding whether or not to stretch the truth.

The Spirit isn't just helping you avoid "big sins." He's forming Christ in you in the smallest decisions.

He's the reason you apologize when you could've made excuses, you deleted that post instead of defending your snark, you stay up listening to a friend instead of checking out with Netflix, you care about becoming the same person in private as you are in public.

That's spiritual maturity. And it's the mark of ethical integrity.

Now let's talk about one more thing; something that rarely gets discussed in conversations about ethics: joy.

Yes, joy. Because believe it or not, walking in the Spirit is not meant to feel like a spiritual root canal. It's not drudgery. It's delight.

Sure, it can be hard. Conviction stings. Surrender stretches us. But the fruit of that obedience? The intimacy with God? The clarity of purpose? That's where the joy lives. Real, sustaining, soul-deep joy.

And that joy becomes your strength.

It helps you say no when everyone else is saying yes, keep you going when no one else notices, forgive when it still hurts, hope when the story feels unfinished.

This isn't just theory. This is life in the Spirit. It's what Jesus was talking about when He said, "My yoke is easy and my burden is light." Not because life itself is easy – but because He's carrying it with you. Because His Spirit is working in you.

And here's the full-circle beauty of it all:

The more you walk with the Spirit, the more you begin to want what God wants. Not just obey it. Desire it.

You stop looking for the minimum obedience required, and you start looking for ways to love well. Serve well. Live honestly. Speak gently. Give generously. Stand boldly.

And when you stumble – and you will – you won't spiral into shame. You'll repent quickly, rest deeply, and rise again with renewed grace. Because the Spirit doesn't condemn. He restores.

So, let's wrap this up in a sentence that's both incredibly freeing and slightly terrifying:

You don't have to figure it all out.

The Holy Spirit will teach you how to live ethically – not in a day but in a lifetime.

He'll guide you moment by moment, choice by choice. He'll give you strength when yours runs out. He'll correct you when you drift, comfort you when you ache, and celebrate every step you take toward Christlikeness – even the small ones.

Because Christian ethics isn't about sin management. It's about Spirit-led transformation.

You're not just avoiding bad behaviour. You're becoming someone beautiful.

And the Spirit is the one making it happen.

You know what's interesting? A lot of people talk about "walking in the Spirit" like it's this mystical experience reserved for missionaries and people who can pray for three hours without checking their phones. But really, it's just regular obedience in step with supernatural help.

It's the whispered "wait" when you're about to rush ahead, the strange sense of peace when everything should feel chaotic, sudden insight that what's being said sounds almost right – but not quite, the pull for someone out of nowhere, or the hesitation when you're about to cut a corner, or the urge to say sorry even though it wasn't "technically" your fault.

That's the Holy Spirit.

Not loud. Not flashy. Just faithful.

Sometimes He uses your conscience. Sometimes He uses Scripture. Sometimes It's just a gut check that makes you pause. But if you've walked with Him long enough, you start recognizing His tone. He doesn't guilt-trip or nag. He doesn't rant or manipulate. He doesn't leave you confused or ashamed. He speaks like Jesus – full of grace and truth.

And if you think you're the only one who struggles to hear Him clearly, you're not. We all do. Even the seasoned saints have days where they ask, "Lord, was that You...or was that just caffeine?"

Thankfully, the Spirit is patient. He doesn't quit talking just because we miss it the first (or fifth) time. He's a better communicator than we are listeners. And He's far more invested in us getting it right than we are.

That means you can relax. You're not walking a moral tightrope with God watching and waiting for you to fall. You're walking a Spirit-led path where grace picks you up every time you stumble.

Now, let's be honest: Spirit-led ethics can make you look strange. You might be the only one in your friend group who doesn't laugh at certain jokes, or turn down opportunities that look amazing, because the Spirit gives you a red flag. Stay loyal to people when the world tells you to cut them off. Give generously when it would be easier to keep. Tell the truth when a lie would save face or choose quiet service over loud recognition. And yes, sometimes you'll look like a fool.

But you'll be a Spirit-filled fool, and there's no safer or stronger place to be, than squarely in the will of God, led by His Spirit, rooted in His Word.

The truth is, this world doesn't need more "nice" Christians. It needs Spirit-led disciples. People who carry the fruit of the Spirit in their actual lives, not just their Instagram bios.

People who can love with patience, speak with kindness, resist temptation, stand for truth, and show compassion. Not because they're naturally good at it, but because the Spirit is at work in them.

And let's talk about this: the Holy Spirit doesn't just help you with doing right. He helps you with receiving grace when you mess up.

Because you will mess up. We all do.

There will be days when you say the thing you shouldn't have said. When you act out of fear instead of faith. When your mouth moves faster than your discernment.

The Holy Spirit doesn't disappear in those moments. He doesn't withhold Himself to "teach you a lesson." He draws near. Convicts. Corrects. And then He walks you through it with gentleness and truth.

And slowly, over time, the mess-ups become fewer. Not because you're perfect, but because you're more aware. More sensitive. More surrendered.

That's what maturity looks like. It's not never failing. It's failing less and rising faster. Knowing where your strength comes from. Walking so closely with the Spirit that you recognize compromise for what it is: a lie that promises freedom but delivers bondage.

The Holy Spirit doesn't just make you holy. He makes you whole.

He heals the bitter places. The scared places. The stubborn, selfish, cynical places. He takes the broken pieces of your past and doesn't just patch them up – He redeems them. He takes your weakness and uses it as a testimony. He takes your pain and births compassion. He takes your failures and transforms them into fuel for someone else's freedom.

You want to know what real Christian ethics looks like?

It looks like people who have been changed from the inside out. People who don't need applause to feel worthy. People who tell the truth even when it hurts. People who love their enemies, forgive their betrayers, and hold the line even when it costs them everything.

And here's the miracle: you can be that person.

Not because you're strong – but because the Spirit is. Because you don't have to manufacture righteousness. You just have to surrender to the One who does.

So, stop striving. Stop white-knuckling your morality like it's the only thing holding your faith together. Stop pretending obedience is something you can perform for God instead of something you walk out with God.

Let the Spirit lead you. He's already at work, speaking, guiding, filling you with power you didn't even know you had.

Power to live differently, love deeply, forgive fully, shine brightly, and endure faithfully.

And most of all, power to look like Jesus, not just in belief but in life. That's what Christian ethics is really about. Not behavior modification. But Spirit-powered transformation. And the best part? He's not done with you yet.

Chapter 6:

The Church as an Ethical Community

So, here's a wild thought: what if church was never meant to be a performance with a coffee bar, but a people with a purpose?

Yea, I know. We all say the church is "not a building, it's the people." But let's be honest – sometimes it feels like a weekly event you attend, critique, and maybe post a highlight reel about if the worship team crushed the songs that day. It's easy to forget that church isn't just where we go. It's who we are. And more than that, it's who we're becoming.

Because here's the thing: the church isn't just a gathering of saved individuals. It's a community designed to live out Christian ethics together.

Not perfectly, but purposely. And painfully sometimes, too. Because people.

But that's what makes it beautiful.

See, ethics doesn't thrive in isolation. You can't practice humility, patience, forgiveness, or selflessness on a desert island. (I mean, maybe you could forgive a coconut for rolling away, but it's not quite the same.)

Christian ethics needs community. Real, awkward, coffee-breath, people-who-sing-off-key community.

But we don't always see it that way.

Sometimes we treat church like a moral lecture series, something we attend to collect better behavior tips. Sometimes we treat it like spiritual entertainment, if the message hits and the music slaps, we're good for the week. Or we treat it like a customer service hub – when it stops "meeting my needs," we switch providers.

But biblically? Church is a covenant family where God shapes us, sharpens us, and sends us.

It's not just a place you come to hear the truth. It's where you come to practice it. With other people who are also trying to figure out what it looks like to love, serve, repent, and grow.

The early church understood this. Not because they had cool branding or clever series titles. But because they were desperate – and devoted.

Acts 2 paints the picture. After the Holy Spirit is poured out, the believers don't just experience personal transformation – they experience communal formation. They devoted themselves to the apostles' teaching, to fellowship, to breaking bread, and to prayer. They shared what they had. They met daily. They worshiped together. They belonged to each other.

They weren't just individuals following Jesus. They were a body, every part needed, every member valuable, every function essential.

And here's where it gets practical for Christian ethics: the church was where their new identity in Christ started changing the way they lived.

They didn't just believe different things they lived in a different way. They just didn't read about generosity; they shared their actual stuff. They didn't preach forgiveness; they reconciled and bore with one another. They didn't attend a service; they became a serving people.

It wasn't polished. It wasn't perfect. But it was powerful.

Because when people truly walk in Christ-centered community, ethics become real-not theoretical. Not abstract. Not "nice ideas to nod at but don't do." Real.

You want to grow in patience? Spend time in a small church group with a guy who asks every single week if the church believes in dinosaurs.

You want to learn forgiveness? Get hurt by someone you trusted in church and then learn to walk out reconciliation instead of revenge.

You want to grow in humility? Volunteer on a setup team where no one knows you're a VP at your job.

These are the places ethics gets real. Not just on the page, but in practice.

But let's be honest – it is not always easy.

Community means commitment. And commitment means people get to see the parts of you that you don't always like seeing yourself. Community means you can't just disappear when things get uncomfortable. It means accountability. Vulnerability. Consistency.

And that's hard in a culture that treats relationships like fast food, cheap, quick, and disposable.

But biblical community isn't a convenience. It's a covenant.

You're not just connected to the church when it benefits you. You're part of the church because you belong to Christ. And that means you have both a role and a responsibility to live out His ethics within His body.

Paul uses the image of a body on purpose. In 1 Corinthians 12, he says the hand can't say to the foot, "I don't need you." And the eye can't say to the ear, "You don't matter." (Imagine if your kidney tried to resign because it felt unappreciated.) Every part matters. Every person matters. Because every believer has been given a measure of the Spirit for the building up of the whole.

You are not just called to be holy for yourself. You're called to grow in holiness for the sake of the people around you.

Your love matters to someone else's healing. Your gentleness matters to someone else's discipleship, and your faithfulness matters to someone else's courage.

And here's the secret: it's often in doing life together that your own spiritual blind spots get revealed and healed.

We grow by friction.

Not the "I'm-starting-a-church-split" kind of friction. But the gentle rub of real relationships where we learn we're not the center of the universe. And that other people's perspectives, wounds, and wisdom have something to teach us.

The church is meant to be the training ground for ethical living – not the showroom floor for people who already have it together.

So, if you're waiting until you're more patient to get involved, or more holy to serve, or more mature to speak up – stop. Jump in. Get messy. Be teachable. Let the community shape you.

Because ethics isn't a solo sport.

It's a group project, but you know, the rare kind where everyone actually does their part.

And the Spirit? He's the glue holding us all together.

Church life has a remarkable way of revealing what we'd rather keep hidden. Maybe you're navigating a misunderstanding with someone who genuinely meant well – but still left a bruise. Or you're dealing with the quiet disappointment of being overlooked when you thought you had something important to offer. Then there are those moments where someone's spiritual growth seems stuck in slow motion, and all your fruit-of-the-Spirit instincts are screaming for a deadline.

These aren't just inconveniences. They're sacred opportunities.

This is where spiritual formation moves from theory to reality. It's not about impressing others with polished virtue, it's about learning to love in the real-world mess of relationships, where grace has to be practiced not just preached.

No seminary textbook can teach you how to forgive like the person who blindsided you with a careless word. There's no online course for learning gentleness through disappointment. These are the kinds of lessons the Holy Spirit teaches in the fellowship hall, and the car ride home, and the text you retype three times before finally pressing send.

And yeah, sometimes people in the church will hurt you. That's not a reason to abandon the church.

It's the invitation to walk out your faith with more depth than comfort ever demanded of you.

Before you grab your metaphorical megaphone to announce your departure or open up a Substack to explain your "journey away from institutional religion," pause. Ask yourself: was I expecting community to do for me what only Christ can?

Even in all her messiness, the church is still the bride of Christ. He doesn't love her because she gets everything right – He loves her because she belongs to Him, He's not looking to swap her out for a trendier option. And if He's not ashamed to call her His, maybe we shouldn't be either.

Now, leadership – yes, it matters. But so does grace. If you're waiting for perfect leaders, you'll be waiting until there is a new heaven and new earth. Until then, the goal isn't flawless performance, it's faithful repentance.

And don't forget this: you don't have to be on a platform to influence a church's integrity. Culture is shaped in quiet moments. A kind word to a newcomer. A prayer over someone struggling. A quiet act of service without fanfare. Those aren't footnotes – they're foundations.

You're not an observer. You're not an extra in God's production. You're part of the story.

When you live with integrity – consistently, even when no one's keeping score. You become the kind of person who doesn't just critique the church. You build it up.

We all want church to feel like home. But even the best homes have leaky faucets and uninvited tensions. So, it shouldn't surprise us when spiritual family brings friction.

And really, that friction is part of how we grow. Not because conflict is ideal, but because comfort rarely produces maturity. When someone pushes your buttons, it's not just an annoyance; it's a mirror. You get to see where your patience ends, where your grace wobbles, and where your pride flares up.

It's uncomfortable, sure. But it's also holy ground.

Growth doesn't always show up in thunderclaps. Sometimes it's just learning not to snap back. Or choosing to listen instead of defend. Or sticking around when your instinct is to pull away.

These aren't dramatic spiritual feats, they're acts of quiet courage. They're the little decisions that slowly train your soul to reflect the One you follow.

The beauty of the church is that it gives you space to become who God already sees in you.

It's where your rough edges bump into other rough edges, and the Spirit smooths them both out. And while we all love the idea of iron sharpening iron, we sometimes forget that sparks fly when it happens.

Still, the sparks are worth it. Because over time, you begin to see just how deeply God uses ordinary relationships to do extraordinary refining.

Even when it's hard.

Especially when it's hard.

If there's anything this world is desperate for, its clarity wrapped in compassion.

People aren't starving for more noise; they're starving for something real. Something rooted, that doesn't shift with the next cultural wave or buckle under public opinion.

And the church, at her best, offers exactly that.

Not through perfect people. But through redeemed ones. People who've been loved deeply enough by Jesus that they can afford to love others with something more durable than niceness. People who aren't afraid to speak truth but have the wisdom to know when to speak it gently, when to stand firm, and when to simply be present without preaching a single word.

That's the ethical witness of the church.

Not shouting louder than culture – but living so differently that culture has to ask why.

You don't need to memorize a script to represent Christ well. You just need to walk in step with the Spirit, and actually mean what you say you believe. The watching world isn't moved by your theological vocabulary. It's moved when you choose faithfulness in the face of fear. When you stay kind in the face of cruelty. When you keep showing up even when you're tired, discouraged, or overlooked.

Church isn't just a place to receive truth – it's a launching pad to live it out. To embody it in the grocery store line, at the office, in your parenting, in your dating life, and on your social media feed. The world needs Christians whose ethics aren't just framed on coffee mugs but carved into their daily habits.

And if you're worried about getting it right all the time – don't be. You wont.

But the beauty of church is that it's not about who's flawless. It's about who's faithful, to repent when you mess up, to reconcile when relationships get strained, and to keep going when spiritual fatigue tempts you to drift.

Community gives you witnesses – not just of your strengths, but of your sanctification.

People who see the real you and choose to walk with you anyway. That's rare. And that's holy.

So, if you're in a church that's trying – maybe not always nailing it but really trying to be faithful – thank God for that. And don't just consume. Contribute. Add your voice, your service, prayers and kindness. It matters more than you know.

Because the church isn't the building.

It's the people who stay.

The ones who don't flee at the first sign of tension. The ones who forgive, grow, wrestle, repent, worship and serve and make space for others to find their footing.

And yes, it's the ones who don't always get credit but are deeply known by the God they serve.

If you want a life that actually reflects the Kingdom – plant yourself among people who are learning to live it out too.

Because at the end of the day, Christian ethics is never meant to be an individual pursuit. It's a shared one. Rooted in love. Anchored in truth. Empowered by grace.

And when that kind of church shows up in a weary world?

It doesn't just make a difference.

It makes disciples.

Chapter 7:

Obedience Without Legalism

Let's be honest, when most people hear the word obedience, it doesn't exactly make them want to throw a party. It sounds like curfews, chore charts, or that voice in your head saying, "Don't eat the cookie," while you're already chewing it.

Then add in the word legalism, and now it just feels like a flashback, to getting side-eyed at church because your skirt wasn't long enough, or because you listened to music with drums in it.

Somewhere along the way, obedience got a bad reputation. Either we treated it like a soul-crushing checklist, or we ditched it entirely in favor of a grace that requires nothing and transforms no one. But Scripture paints a different picture. Obedience isn't the enemy of grace. It's the evidence of it.

The tension we feel is real, though. We've all met the person who seems to have the entire book of Leviticus memorized but somehow missed the part about kindness. They tithe to the penny, quote KJV like Shakespeare, and are deeply concerned about the length of your sleeves. But if you sat next to them during communion, you'd feel more judged than loved.

That's not holiness. That's legalism in a Sunday suit.

On the other hand, we've also seen the version of faith where obedience is optional.

Where God loves you "just as you are" – and never seems to ask for anything different. Where the only sin that gets called out is making someone feel uncomfortable.

That's not grace. That's a permission slip for spiritual apathy.

So how do we find the balance? How do we obey without becoming rigid? How do we pursue holiness without becoming the Holiness Police?

Here's where we begin: Obedience is a response to relationship, not a replacement for it.

You don't obey God to earn His love. You obey Him because you already have it.

And when that sinks in, when obedience is rooted in delight instead of duty, you stop obsessing over rules and start caring about the heart behind them. You're not trying to "check off" righteousness. You're learning to walk in step with the One who made you righteous.

You see this in Jesus' ministry over and over. He didn't come to smash sinners with law. He came to fulfill it and free people to live it. He didn't applaud the Pharisees for their rule-keeping; He called them out for their lack of love. But He also didn't lower the standard of righteousness to make it more palatable. He raised it higher than anyone expected – and then gave His Spirit to make it possible.

That's the key. Obedience, apart from the Spirit, becomes oppression. But obedience empowered by the Spirit becomes joy.

The problem with legalism isn't that it cares too much about obedience, it's that it cares about the wrong kind.

Legalism wants performance without posture. It wants outward compliance with zero heart change. It's the kid who cleans their room but mutters under their breath the whole time and kicks the laundry basket. Technically obedient? Sure. But joyful? Not even close.

And that's what Jesus consistently challenged. The Pharisees weren't wrong to pursue moral lives; they were wrong in thinking that moral lives made them righteous. They saw the law as a ladder to climb their way to heaven. Jesus came and turned that ladder into a cross.

Obedience in the kingdom is never about proving your worth. It's about reflecting God's character. It doesn't scream, "Look what I've done!" It quietly says, "This is who I belong to."

But let's not swing the other way and assume that if we avoid legalism, we're good. Sometimes what we call freedom is actually just flesh in disguise. Just because obedience isn't required to earn grace doesn't mean it's optional once we have it.

Grace is not get-out-of-holiness-free card. It's the divine power to actually become holy.

That's why Jesus didn't just say, "If you love Me, you'll sing to Me." Or "If you love Me, you'll repost My verses on social media." He said, "If you love Me, keep My commandments." John 14:15

There's not wiggle room there. Love leads to obedience. Not as a demand, but as a desire. Real love always leads to real action.

So, if we're serious about walking in Christian ethics, we have to ask: Are we obeying God because we love Him, or are we obeying to look like we love Him?"

The difference might not show up on the outside. But it always shows up in your spirit.

When obedience flows from love, it produces fruit. There's joy, peace, humility. You're more aware of your need for God, not less. You become more patient with others, not more critical. You walk with confidence, not comparison.

When obedience flows from fear or performance, it produces pride or burnout, or both. You either feel superior to others who "aren't trying as hard," or you feel like a failure who never quite measures up.

One path leads to rest.

The other leads to resentment.

The Spirit is always guiding us toward the first.

Sometimes legalism doesn't knock on the front door, it slips in through the side window, wearing a Jesus T-shirt and holding a checklist. It shows up not just in strict rule-keepers, but in well-meaning believers trying to be "good Christians."

It's the voice that says, "I didn't read my Bible this morning – God must be disappointed in me."

Or "I missed church last week – maybe that's why things are falling apart."

Or "I'd never wear that to worship. Can you believe she did?"

And just like that, obedience turns into superstition. Holiness becomes performance. The Christian lie becomes a tightrope walk, and God becomes the disappointed coach on the sidelines.

But that's not how Jesus operates. He's not waiting to pounce on your every misstep. He's walking with you, guiding you with gentleness and truth. The Spirit doesn't shame you into holiness. He shepherds you into it.

That's why it's so important to listen to His voice. Not just when you're praying, but when you're posting. When you're budgeting.

When you're standing at a crossroads between what feels comfortable and what you know is right.

Obedience doesn't mean you'll always feel like it. Let's be honest – there are days when "love your enemies" feels more like "tolerate them silently while replaying a fake argument in your head." But this is where Spirit-empowered obedience gets beautifully real.

Because the Holy Spirit doesn't just give you a spiritual to-do list. He gives you new desires. He doesn't just say, "Be patient." He shapes you into someone who wants to be patient. He doesn't just say, "Forgive them again." He softens your heart so you're able to. He doesn't just say, "Obey." He empowers you to obey with joy.

You're not forcing fruit to grow – you're abiding in the Vine. And that fruit starts showing up in the places where obedience used to feel like drudgery.

It doesn't mean it's easy. It means it's no longer all on your shoulders.

Legalism makes you carry the weight of your righteousness like a badge you earned. The Spirit lets you wear Christ's righteousness like a robe you were gifted. One says, "Look what I did." The other says, "Look who He is."

And that changes everything.

When obedience is rooted in identity instead of insecurity you stop striving. You stop comparing. You stop needing everyone else to affirm that you're "doing it right." You just walk. Steady. Simply. Obedient. Free.

That's when your ethics becomes alive – not dry, not robotic, but radiant. Not because you nailed all the rules. But because you stayed close to the One who loves you too much to let you settle for sin.

You know you're growing in obedience when it starts interfering with your preferences.

It's one thing to obey God in the abstract. To nod along in church and say things like, "Amen" or "So true." It's another thing entirely to obey Him when it's Friday night and everyone else is doing something sketchy-but-social, and you're over here Googling, "Can I glorify God at a brewery trivia night?"

This is where obedience gets legs. Where theology moves out of your Bible app and into your calendar, your conversations, your choices.

And here's the truth: real obedience will cost you something.

Sometimes it costs you conversation you really wanted to have...you know that delicious, morally gray bit of gossip disguised as "concern."

Sometimes it costs you comfort, because integrity won't let you fudge the numbers, bend the truth, or flirt with that line you know God already drew.

And let's not kid ourselves – there are days when obedience feels about as convenient as a flat tire in the rain. But that's exactly when it matters most.

Obedience without legalism isn't about jumping through hoops to prove you're spiritual. It's about listening to the Spirit when He says, "Not that way. Follow Me instead."

And it happens in all kinds of unspectacular moments:

When you speak gently instead of winning the argument, you delete the comment you really wanted to post, you keep your promise, even though it no longer benefits you, you forgive without a dramatic monologue.

No one claps. No one gives you a trophy, but heaven notices.

That's the beautiful thing about Spirit-led obedience. It rarely feels flashy. It often feels small. But over time, it reshapes your entire life.

Legalism demands that every decision be scrutinized under a microscope: "Is this allowed? Is that okay? What would Sister So-and-So think?"

But grace-fueled obedience is relational. It asks, "What would please the heart of the One who loves me most?"

It's not a transaction. It's trust. And that trust gets tested in the moments you weren't planning for.

Like when you have to walk away from a dating relationship that you know is pulling you away from God – but your heart hasn't gotten the memo. When you're telling the truth means losing face, losing friends, or losing a promotion. When you show up to serve again even though no one's thanked you since 2019.

These are the moments where obedience looks less like a victory lap, and more like a quiet "yes" in the dark.

But here's what you'll discover: the more you say yes to God, the more you start wanting to.

Not because you're becoming more disciplined, but because you're becoming more surrendered.

The Holy Spirit reshapes your "want to." And suddenly, the things you used to white-knuckle, you now walk in – imperfectly, but freely.

Obedience becomes less about willpower and more about joy. Less about proving something, more about abiding in Someone.

You'll still mess up. You'll still need grace daily. But you'll find that grace isn't just a safety net – it's a launchpad. It gives you room to grow without fear of falling out of favor.

So yes, obedience might cost you some things. But it gives you far more: peace, clarity, trust, intimacy with God, and a quiet, anchored soul in a world full of noise.

You can't put that on a checklist.

But you can live it – one Spirit-led yes at a time.

You know what's wild?

You can follow every visible "Christian rule," serve on three committees, carry a genuine leather King James, and still be spiritually dry as toast.

Because fruit doesn't grow from effort alone. It grows from connection.

Jesus didn't say, "Try harder to be holy." He said, "Abide in Me." Stay close. Stay connected. Stay rooted. That's where the fruit shows up.

But here's where it gets tricky: fruit doesn't always look like what people expect.

Legalism tends to obsess over the "easy-to-measure" stuff. Things like church attendance, tithing totals, dress code compliance, or how many Bible trivia answers you can rattle off without using the table of contents.

And don't get me wrong – those things can be great. But you can fake them. You can wear spiritual busyness like a disguise while your soul is quietly starving.

Real fruit, though? It's harder to fake it. It shows up when no one's watching.

Like when you pause before reacting. When your words get softer. When the old temptations lose some of their grip, and you realize you'd rather please God than impress people. That's fruit.

It's when your instincts start changing.

You used to fire off that sarcastic text without a second thought – now the Holy Spirit hits you with a "let's maybe not..." You used to compare yourself to every other believer on social media – now you're praying for them instead of scrolling with resentment. You used to love being right – now you're learning how to love being kind.

That's not moral window dressing. That's transformation. That's obedience coming alive from the inside out.

And let's be honest: fruit doesn't always grow fast. You're not going to wake up tomorrow with a halo and the patience of Job just because you had one holy Tuesday. Some days feel like slow progress. Some days feel like no progress. But here's the thing about fruit, it takes time, but it does grow if the tree stays rooted.

So, if you're wondering whether your obedience is working, don't just ask, "Am I doing the right things?" Ask, "Am I becoming more like Jesus?"

That's the goal. Not a polished spiritual resume. Not a reputation for being "one of the good ones." Just quiet, steady, Spirit-shaped character.

The world doesn't need more Christians who know the rules. It needs more who bear the fruit.

Love that's inconvenient. Joy that's circumstantial. Peace that doesn't hinge on control. Patience that endures real people. Kindness that surprises strangers. Goodness that runs deep. Faithfulness that stays when it's hard. Gentleness that doesn't get loud. Self-control that doesn't scream but stands.

None of that comes from legalism. That's what the Spirit grows in surrendered soil.

So, if you're obeying – and you feel unseen, uncelebrated, unflashy – don't panic. You might be doing it exactly right.

Because obedience isn't about the spotlight. It's about the roots.

Stay connected. Stay faithful. Keep watering what God planted.

Fruit's coming.

You've probably seen both kinds of spiritual burnout.

One version looks like someone who tried so hard to be "good" that they snapped. They checked every box, never missed a Sunday, always looked "together" – until one day they just...disappeared. Ghosted the church. Unfollowed all the Christian accounts. Stopped answering texts. When asked what happened, they quietly mutter, "I just couldn't do it anymore."

The other version? It's the person who got so allergic to legalism that they ditched every spiritual discipline like it was a cursed relic from 1997. They say things like, "It's not about doing stuff – it's just about being." Which sounds poetic...until their life looks indistinguishable from someone who doesn't know Jesus at all.

Both are tragic. And neither is what Jesus meant when He said, "My yoke is easy, and My burden is light."

Because real obedience is sustainable. Not because it's effortless – but because it's empowered.

You're not meant to gut your way through the Christian life. You're meant to walk it with Someone.

That "easy yoke" Jesus talked about? It's not a hammock. It's not passive. It's not coasting through life with a Bible verse on your screensaver and hoping osmosis will sanctify you.

It's active obedience – with supernatural help.

It means waking up each day, not with panic or guilt, but with trust: "God, I'm Yours. Shape me. Lead me. Correct me when I drift. And give me the strength to obey – especially when it's hard."

That posture? That's freedom.

It's not the freedom to do whatever you want and slap a "Jesus loves me anyway" sticker on it.

It's the freedom to walk with God, without the pressure to perform and without the permission to coast.

It's staying close to Him – not because you're afraid He'll leave, but because you've learned there's nowhere better to be.

And when you mess up – and you will – it's not the end of the road. It's another chance to walk in grace. Real grace. Not the kind that excuses sin, but the kind that destroys it with kindness and picks you back up with mercy.

Obedience doesn't make you less dependent on grace. It makes you more aware of how much you need it.

It's not the graduation from grace. It's the evidence that grace is working.

So, how do you stay faithful without falling into fear or laziness?

Simple – stay near Jesus.

Let the Word remind you of who you are. Let prayer keep your heart soft. Let correction humble you. Let grace carry you whenever your strength runs out.

And let the Holy Spirit keep you walking – not perfectly, but faithfully.

Because legalism will keep you anxious. License will leave you empty. But obedience, real Spirit-shaped obedience?

That'll make you holy.

And holy people don't look stiff or superior.

They look like Jesus.

Chapter 8:
Grace, Failure, and the Ethical Life

If Christian ethics were a board game, most of us would be disqualified in the first five minutes for losing the rulebook, accidentally flipping the board, and yelling at the dice.

That's the problem with trying to live a morally upright life while still being a human with emotions, temptations, and the occasional passive-aggressive group text. You want to live right. You really do. But then Tuesday hits. Or your boss does the thing again. Or someone cuts you off in traffic with a Jesus fish on the bumper.

And just like that, your holiness goes on lunch break.

That's where grace steps in – not as a spiritual mop for your mess, but as the foundation under your feet. Grace is the only reason you can live a truly ethical life in the first place. Not because it lowers the bar, but because it keeps you from drowning when you miss it.

Now, failure isn't a comfortable word in Christian circles. We'd rather say, "fell short," "struggled," or the classic "had a moment." But the truth is, we all blow it sometimes – spectacularly, repeatedly, and, if we're honest, sometimes with a weird mix of regret and relief. Regret, because we know better. Relief, because we finally stopped pretending, we don't need grace as much as the person we were silently judging last week.

Failure in the ethical life doesn't mean you've forfeited your faith. It means you're a candidate for grace. The real kind. Not the Instagram version that says, "nobody's perfect," with a soft filter, but the rugged blood-bought grace that calls you to repent and restores you anyway.

What most people don't understand is that grace isn't soft. It's not the spiritual equivalent of, "Aw, don't worry about it." It's fierce. It's stubborn. It won't let you sit in your failure, but it also won't kick you out of the family when you fall. It calls you higher – after it picks you up.

That's why ethical failure – when seen through the lens of grace – doesn't have to lead to hiding. It can lead to healing. Think of Peter. He literally denied Jesus to a middle-school-aged girl by a fire, and Jesus still reinstated him with fish and breakfast. Jesus didn't toss Peter's resume. He fed him and reminded him who he really is.

Grace tells the truth about sin and then tells a bigger truth about your identity in Christ.

And this is where Christian ethics differs radically from every other moral framework. Other systems say, "You failed, so you are a failure." The gospel says, "You failed, so come back to grace – and let's try again, together."

Somewhere along the way, "grace" became one of those Christian words that gets tossed around like confetti at a youth group lock-in.

You see it printed on mugs, painted on brush-script over reclaimed wood, and tattooed on wrists, sometimes with a butterfly. And while none of that is inherently bad (tattoo responsibly), it's not the full story.

Because grace, at its core, is not just something you receive, it's something that rearranges you.

It's not a vibe. It's not a blanket you curl up in when you feel guilty. Grace is power. It's the undeserved, unearned, unstoppable favor of God that doesn't just cover your sin – it calls you out of it. It doesn't say, "You're fine." It says, "You're forgiven – and free."

Now, let's be clear: grace doesn't make sin less serious. It just makes redemption possible.

In fact, if grace doesn't shake you a little, if it doesn't make you pause and say, "Wait, I get to come back from that?" Then you probably haven't seen the real thing yet. Real grace is scandalous. It welcomes the prodigal home while the older brother is still composing his angry Facebook post.

But here's the twist, grace isn't soft on sin. It just doesn't see it as the end of your story.

Grace says, "Yes, that was sin. No, you're not done." It's what reached out to Peter when he was sinking in shame.

It's what met Paul – formerly Saul – on a dusty road with a blinding light and a holy interruption. It's what brought you and me into this whole thing in the first place.

And it's not a one-time rescue.

You don't graduate from grace. It's not the training wheels of Christian life that you ditch once you get "serious" about God. It's the fuel. The engine. The air in your spiritual lungs. The reason you can repent without running away. The reason you can be honest about your failures without drowning in them.

Legalism tries to earn what grace gives away. Shame tries to bury what grace redeems. But grace? Grace walks into your mess and stays. It pulls up a chair at the table and says, "Let's talk."

It's not lenient. It's loyal. And because of that, it's life-altering.

Think of it this way: If the law shows you where the path is, grace is what picks you up when you fall off it, dusts you off, and walks beside you as you try again. Grace doesn't lower the bar of ethics – it gives you the strength to reach for it without fear of rejection, every time you miss.

That's why it's possible to live with conviction and compassion at the same time.

Grace lets you be honest about sin without living in shame over it. It lets you hold to truth without becoming harsh or smug.

It's grace that makes repentance possible, not just as a moment, but as a lifestyle.

Because in this ethical journey, you're going to need grace often. Probably before lunch.

But that's okay. Because grace isn't running out. You're not going to wake up one morning and find God saying, "Yea, about that...turns out you used your last mercy token yesterday. You're on your own."

No, Scripture says His mercies are new every morning. Like spiritual fresh laundry – clean, warm, and ready for you to try again.

So don't treat grace like a back-up plan. Treat it like the actual plan.

That's what God intended all along.

We don't love talking about failure in church.

We love testimonies, sure – but only once there's a bow on top. We like the neat ending: "I was a mess, but now I'm a mentor." We clap when someone says, "I used to struggle," because it feels safe, past tense. What we don't know how to handle is someone standing up and saying, "Actually, I'm still in it. I haven't licked this yet. I'm walking out repentance in real time."

But that's where real grace does its best work.

Failure, as uncomfortable as it is, might be one of the most honest parts of the ethical life. It tells you that your theology isn't just theory. It shows you where your roots actually are. It exposes whether your faith is about control or surrender. And sometimes, it teaches you more in one stumble than a hundred sermons ever could.

Don't get me wrong, God never wants you to fail. But He's also not surprised when you do.

And when you do, He's not standing at the edge of the cliff yelling, "How could you?" He's already climbed down into the ravine saying, "Let's go."

Failure has a way of humbling you in all the right ways. It turns your spiritual volume down. It makes you less interested in managing your image, and more interested in cultivating integrity. It teaches you how to pray without pretending, and it helps you look at other struggling people and say, not with condescension, but with compassion, "I get it. I've been there too."

You can't teach that from a platform. You learn it face-first on the carpet, asking God to meet you in the rubble.

Here's the thing: ethical failure isn't disqualifying, it's revealing. It shows you where you're trying to manage sin instead of killing it.

It shows you where you still believe lies about yourself, about God, about what matters most. It reveals the cracks in your foundation, so the Holy Spirit can start reinforcing them with truth.

And that's good news.

Because if failure reveals something, then failure can teach something. It can teach you humility. Dependency. Honesty. It can deepen your compassion and quiet your arrogance. It can move you from knowing about grace to actually living inside of it.

But only if you let it.

You see, failure that leads to repentance is redemptive. But failure that leads to shame or self-pity? That's just pride in disguise. It's still focused on you – on how disappointed you are in yourself, how far you fell, how you should've known better. But grace gently interrupts that monologue and says, "Hey. Let's not waste this. Let's learn."

And when that becomes your posture, your ethical life doesn't become perfect – it becomes resilient.

You don't bounce back because you're strong. You bounce back because you've learned that God's strength doesn't disappear just because you slipped.

Failure can either harden your heart or soften it. It can make you bitter or make you wise. And honestly, the difference is usually whether you try to hide it or bring it into the light.

God isn't looking for spotless performance. He's looking for surrendered hearts.

So, next time you fail – and you will – don't run, don't spin, and don't build a wall of shame. Walk back into the presence of God, hands open, heart honest, and say, "Okay. What now, Lord?"

You'll be amazed at what He can grow out of ground you thought was ruined.

That's the strange pressure that exists in Christian spaces – especially the ones with good coffee and a stylish Instagram presence. It's the unspoken expectation that even when you're falling apart, you still need to look..." together." Not sinless, exactly – just sinning in away that photographs well. Clean struggles only. Acceptable flaws, preferably packaged with a Bible verse and a lesson learned.

And it's exhausting.

We've created a church culture that's great at celebrating deliverance, but kind of awkward with dependence. We're comfortable saying, "I used to struggle with anger." But say, "I'm still fighting it – and I yelled at my kids this morning," and the room goes quiet.

Eye contact disappears. People start asking if you've tried journaling more.

But grace only works if you actually bring your mess to the table. And not just the leftovers. The raw stuff. The ugly stuff. The stuff that doesn't have a testimony tied up in a bow – yet.

Living ethically in a world obsessed with appearances means doing something incredibly countercultural: being honest.

Not performative. Not polished. Not "I'm fine, just busy." Honest.

And not just with God – though that's where it starts. But also, with the people around you. The real kind of confession, where you don't filter the sin to make yourself look humble. Where you don't disguise a boast as a "prayer request." Where you tell the truth and trust grace to catch you.

It's hard. But it's holy.

And let's face it – everyone's pretending to some degree. Social media has made it easy to curate the illusion of faithfulness without walking in it. You can post a verse and still not forgive your spouse. You can share a worship song and still lie to your boss. You can "love Jesus" in pixels and still be bitter in person.

Grace doesn't ask you to pretend. It asks you to repent.

And the church is supposed to be the safest place to do that.

Unfortunately, it hasn't always been. Some of the deepest wounds come from communities that preached grace and practiced shame. Where your image mattered more than your healing. Where vulnerability got you shunned instead of supported.

But here's the good news: even when the church gets it wrong, God still gets it right. He still honors the honest. He still draws near to the broken-hearted. And He still builds strong, holy lives out of people who come to Him, not with a resume – but with a real need for mercy.

So, what does it look like to live this way?

It looks like walking into church and not faking it. It looks like telling your small group, "Actually, I'm struggling right now." It looks like confessing a sin before it turns into a stronghold. It looks like letting someone pray for you when your voice is too tired to pray for yourself.

This kind of honesty doesn't make you less holy. It makes you more dependent – and that's where holiness actually grows.

Pretending protects your pride. Honesty protects your soul.

So, if you're living in the tension between grace and failure, stop worrying about your image. Stop curating your testimony. Just tell the truth. Be real. Be repentant. Be redeemed.

It's not always pretty.

But it's always worth it.

We don't usually think about grace as something that trusts us.

We think about us trusting grace, relying on it, falling into it, clinging to it when everything else breaks down. And yes, that's absolutely true. But there's another side too. Grace isn't just something we receive. It's something we steward.

Because grace, when it really takes root, doesn't just forgive. It transforms.

It doesn't hand you a spiritual "get out of jail free" card so you can go back to business as usual. It hands you a new life – and trusts you live it. Not perfectly. But faithfully. Fully. In the open.

And as you keep walking through failure, through repentance, through growth, you start becoming the kind of person grace can trust.

That doesn't mean sinless. It doesn't mean impressive. It means surrendered. It means available.

It means that when grace shows up in your life, it finds a heart that says, "Whatever You want, Lord – I'm in."

And that's a powerful place to live from.

It means grace isn't constantly chasing you down with reminders. You're already listening. Already turning. Already asking the Holy Spirit what's next.

You're not obeying because you're afraid to fall, you're obeying because grace has changed your appetite.

You're not white-knuckling your ethics, you're walking in step with the Spirit.

You're not hiding from your failures, you're learning from them, growing through them, and testifying because of them.

And gradually, beautifully, you become the kind of person God can entrust with more. More influence. More compassion. More wisdom. More weight.

Not because you're stronger. But because you know exactly where your strength ends and where His begins.

That's the ethical life. Not pristine. Not perfect. But possible. Because grace doesn't just erase your past, it reshapes your future.

It keeps calling. Keeps lifting. Keeps inviting you to live not from fear, but from freedom.

And that's a life the world can't fake – and desperately needs to see.

So, keep going.

Keep failing forward. Keep repenting honestly. Keep receiving mercy like it's fresh every morning, because it is. And keep living like grace is more than a concept.

Because it is.

It's a Person.

It's a power.

And it's the reason you're still becoming exactly who God created you to be.

Chapter 9:

Discipleship and
the Daily Decisions

If you've made it this far – through moral law, legalism, grace, failure, Scripture, and everything in between – then congratulations. You're now officially ready for the hardest part of Christian ethics.

The part where you wake up on a Wednesday morning, stare at your crusty coffee pot, and try to figure out what discipleship looks like in real life.

Not in theory. Not in the abstract. Not on a retreat with worship music and catered snacks. But in your actual life – with laundry, tension, deadlines, group texts, and that co-worker who thinks, "boundaries" are a type of snack food.

Because this, right here, is where discipleship happens.

It's not just the mountaintop moments. It's the Wednesday morning moments. It's the choice to be faithful when no one's looking. To be honest when it'd be easier not to be. To be patient when you'd rather be passive-aggressive.

Discipleship is not a title you earn after a certain number of mission trips or theology books. It's a way of life. It's following Jesus, step by step, in the small things. It's letting Him into your reactions, your rhythms, and your calendar.

And yes, it's slower than we'd like.

Modern life has trained us to think in soundbites and shortcuts. Click here. Swipe there. Get the results. But God's not in a hurry. He's not trying to microwave your sanctification. He walks. He teaches. He transforms. Slowly. Personally. Daily.

The problem is, we often look for clarity before obedience.

We want a five-year plan with biblical footnotes. We want confirmation texts from heaven. We want to know exactly where this is going before we start following. But that's not usually how discipleship works.

Jesus didn't hand His disciples a map. He just said, "Follow Me."

And they did. With blisters, doubts, confusion, arguments, and occasional overconfidence (looking at you, Peter). But they kept walking. Kept trusting. Kept growing.

That's what discipleship still looks like.

It's easy to romanticise discipleship until you realize, it's mostly made up of tiny decisions no one claps for.

There's no background music when you choose to hold your tongue in a tense conversation. No spiritual confetti falls from the ceiling when you apologize first.

No fanfare when you choose to read Scripture instead of scrolling for the 42nd time that day. Just you, Jesus and a string of quiet choices that slowly shape the kind of person you're becoming.

Because the ethical life isn't built in the big moments. It's forged in the little ones – when you decide not to embellish the story to sound cooler, or when you turn off the movie you know is numbing your soul, or when you pick up the phone and call the person you've been avoiding for months.

That's discipleship.

It's not about living perfectly – it's about living present. Present to the Spirit. Present to conviction. Present to the people around you, even when they make you want to retreat into a "Jesus and snacks only" bunker.

Following Jesus doesn't mean you suddenly become immune to selfishness. It just means you become quicker to notice it, and slower to let it win.

You start recognizing the little nudges:

"Hey, maybe don't send that text."

"Maybe give instead of hoard this time."

"Maybe listen instead of defending your ego again."

And you learn to respond, not out of guilt, but out of relationship.

Discipleship isn't about living a life that looks impressive. It's about living a life that's aligned.

And alignment doesn't mean rigidity. It means responsiveness. It means you start asking better questions – less about what you can do, and more about what reflects Christ in you.

So, when you're standing in the grocery line and someone cuts in front of you, the question becomes less about who's right, and more about who you're becoming.

When your friend says something that bruises your pride, the question shifts from "How can I win this?" to "How can I love well here?"

When temptation comes knocking – and let's be clear, it will – the issue isn't whether you're a "good Christian" if you resist. It's whether your heart is learning to want what Jesus wants, even when it's costly.

Discipleship is what happens when grace starts changing your reflexes.

And the good news? You don't have to get it right every time for it to count.

God isn't grading you on moral test scores.

He's growing you into someone who bears fruit in the real world, where obedience doesn't always feel dramatic – but it is deeply significant.

You're not building a brand. You're becoming a disciple.

And the more you walk with Jesus, the more your daily decisions begin to look like His. Quiet. Consistent. Full of truth and grace.

You know what makes all this daily obedience possible?

It's not grit. It's not willpower. It's not some secret morning routine that only the "super spiritual" have discovered (although coffee doesn't hurt). The thing that makes daily discipleship actually doable – and even joyful – is relationship.

Real, living, day-in-day-out relationship with Jesus.

Because when you're walking with someone you love and trust, obedience stops feeling like obligation and starts to feel like alignment. You're not just trying to "do the right thing," you're trying to stay close. You're not just avoiding sin; you're moving toward Someone.

That's what Jesus was getting at when He said, "Abide in Me."

Not "check in with Me on Sundays." Not "come find Me when life explodes." Abide. Stay. Live here.

That's where the real transformation happens. Not from a distance. Not in a moral vacuum. But in closeness. In communion. In walking through the ordinary and learning how to see it as sacred because He's in it.

The ethical life isn't about getting better at managing behaviour. It's about becoming someone who wants what Jesus wants, because you know Him.

And here's the truth: if you try to follow Jesus at a distance, it won't work. You'll burn out. You'll start thinking the point is just behaviour modification with a religious filter. You'll miss the joy, the intimacy, the laughter, the peace that comes from walking side by side, with the One who actually knows how to live this life and offers to walk it with you.

Daily decisions are the fruit of daily dependence.

When you wake up and pray, not because it's a checkbox, but because you need Him. When you open the Word, not to impress anyone, but to be reminded of who God is, and who you are in Him. When you stop in the middle of a stressful moment and breathe, "Lord, help me respond like You would."

That's the real stuff. That's the discipleship in motion.

It's not about being the most impressive Christian in the room. It's about being the most surrendered one.

It's not about perfection. It's about presence.

And the more time you spend with Jesus, the more daily decisions start to look like His. Generous, compassionate, honest, courageous, and rooted.

You won't always get it right. You'll still mess up, still forget, still get distracted. But every time you come back, every time you recenter, you're becoming someone who reflects Christ not just in the "big moments," but in the daily, dusty ones.

And that's where the real ethical life lives. In the grocery store. At your desk. In the awkward family dinner. In the waiting. In the joy. In the deeply ordinary places where your decision either echo heaven...or just echo your flesh.

The difference? Relationship.

Walk with Him. Talk to Him. Stay close.

It changes everything.

By now, you've walked through moral law, obedience, Scripture, grace, failure, and a dozen other themes that may have left your spiritual brain doing gymnastics. But here's the through-line, the steady thread holding it all together.

Discipleship isn't about collecting theological information.

It's about becoming someone new, day by day, moment by moment, choice by choice.

Every chapter in this book has been pushing us toward that. Not toward some grand moral achievement, but towards a life deep, abiding faithfulness. Toward a character that isn't performative but rooted. Toward ethics that aren't just intellectual but incarnational – lived out in the body, in the real world, among real people.

Because the Christian life isn't just about believing the right things. It's about letting those beliefs change how you respond when your toddler spills milk for the third time before 9 a.m. Or when someone slanders you online and your fingers are twitching to fire back. Or when no one is watching, and you get to choose between honesty and an easier story.

That's where everything we've studied comes home.

That's where the authority of Scripture meets your browser history. Where the Sermon on the Mount meets your budget. Where the grace you believe in meets the person who keeps hurting you.

Christian ethics aren't meant to float above your life like a theology cloud. They're meant to get dirt under their nails. To live in your car, your kitchen, your workplace, your phone habits.

Because if ethics don't shape your real decisions, what are they shaping?

Discipleship is what happens when everything you believe about God starts showing up in how you treat your neighbor. Your enemies, your spouse, your own weary soul.

It's not glamorous. It's not always clean but it is holy.

And what's more, it's exactly the kind of life Jesus modeled.

He didn't live in a monastery. He didn't isolate Himself with scrolls and snacks (although that's tempting). He walked among the people. He spoke to outcasts. He cooked breakfast for failures. He corrected His disciples when they got it wrong (often). And He invited them to watch – really watch – how He lived.

And now He invites us to do the same.

Not the "fake it till we make it." But to walk with Him until we reflect Him.

That's the heartbeat of this whole book – and this whole life.

So, don't leave these pages thinking discipleship is just a concept you studied. Let it be a calling you live.

Discipleship doesn't end with a finished book or a perfectly highlighted Bible. It's not a certificate you hang on the wall, or a season you graduate from once life calms down. It's a lifestyle. A rhythm. A way of being in the world that says, day after day, "Jesus, You lead – I'll follow."

And some days? You'll follow well.

You'll respond with grace when you're tired, speak truth when it costs something, forgive when your flesh says, "absolutely not." And those days are beautiful.

Other days?

You'll miss it. You'll revert, snap, doubt. You'll sit in your car wondering if any of this is working.

But that doesn't disqualify you.

That's the journey. And Jesus is in all of it.

Not just the mountaintop victories, but the Tuesday failures.

Not just the big spiritual highs, but the boring, in-between moments when you still choose Him. When you keep saying yes. When you keep showing up. When you repent quickly, forgive freely, give generously, and live openly.

That's the ethical life: not pristine perfection, but persistent discipleship.

And here's the thing: it matters.

It matters in a world that's drowning in compromise and craving clarity. It matters in families that are breaking under pressure and looking for hope. It matters in churches that need less performance and more humility. It matters in friendships, boardrooms, grocery aisles, and social media feeds.

Because people may never ask you about your theology of sanctification – but they will notice if you're kind when it's inconvenient. Honest when it's unpopular. Gentle when everyone else is sarcastic.

That's the witness.

That's the fruit.

That's how we love God with all our heart, soul, mind, and strength – by trusting Him with the decisions that no one but Him might ever see.

So here we are.

Nine chapters in. Still imperfect. Still in progress. But maybe – just maybe – more committed than ever to letting our faith shape the way we live, not just the way we talk.

Not because we're trying to impress anyone.

But because we've seen what grace can do.

We've felt what the Spirit can transform.

And we believe that even in a loud, broken, cynical world...obedience still matters. Truth still matters. Jesus still changes everything.

And the next decision you make?

It matters too.

So go walk with Him. Not in fear. Not in striving. But in freedom.

One step.

One moment.

One decision at a time.

Epilogue

So, here we are. The end of Volume I. If you're like most people, you've probably got a mix of thoughts swirling around your head:

"I should really go back and re-read that chapter on grace."

"Did I accidentally become a theologian?"

"Where was this book when I was 19 and making every moral decision based on vibes and caffeine?"

You're not alone.

Writing this wasn't about laying down a law you could never live up to. It was about lifting up a Savior who already has. Every chapter, every sentence, every awkward long metaphor was aimed at one thing: helping you live what you believe – ethically, joyfully, and faithfully.

Because the world doesn't need more perfect Christians.

It needs more honest ones.

People who wrestle with God in the quiet and still choose obedience when no one claps for it. People who repent quickly, forgive deeply, and walk in the kind of grace that doesn't just sound nice – but actually changes them.

You're not expected to get it all right. You're not expected to graduate from grace. You're invited – daily, hourly, sometimes minute-by-minute – to follow Jesus in the middle of your real life. And that's where Christian ethics lie. Not in theory. In the kitchen. On the highway. In your inbox. In the tension between what you want and what's holy.

You'll blow it sometimes. Good. Because that's when you remember that righteousness was never about your resume anyway. It was about the One who gave you His.

So, take a deep breath. Close the book. And don't wait for the perfect moment to start living differently. You already are.

With every choice to love when it's hard, to tell the truth when it's costly, to stay faithful when it's inconvenient, you are living the ethical life. One tiny decision at a time.

And you're not doing it alone.

You've got the Spirit in you. You've got the Word beside you. And you've got a Savior ahead of you who already finished the hardest part.

Now go live like it.

We'll pick up the rest of the story in Volume II.

Until then – stay rooted, stay real, and stay in grace.

- The End (for now).

Author Bio

Kathrin Shaffer is a Bible-loving, tea-fueled writer who believes Christian ethics doesn't have to be dry, dusty, or delivered with a furrowed brow. With a heart for truth and a sense of humor about how messy obedience can be, she writes to encourage real people in their real-life walk with Jesus.

When she's not deep in Scripture or knee-deep in grace, Kathrin is probably wrangling her dogs, laughing at her own jokes, or having a theological debate with her dog; Sergeant (who remains unconvinced). Her passion is helping believers live faithfully – not flawlessly – as they grow in holiness, one – sometimes clumsy step at a time.

Christian Ethics: Volume I – Right-ish is the first in a series designed to explore the practical, biblical, and sometimes hilariously hard journey of becoming more like Christ. Because holiness is not about having it all together, it's about walking with the One who does.

You can find other books written by Kathrin on Amazon or on her website Kathrinshaffer.com.

The King's Wisdom: Biblical Leadership Principles for Modern Business

Living the Word: How to Implement the Bible into Everyday Life

Beauty for Ashes: Walking Through Grief with God

Proverbs 31 Woman: New Christian Women Transitioning from Secular Life to Biblical Womanhood